American History
on the Screen

Film and Video Resource

Wendy S. Wilson and Gerald H. Herman

User's Guide
to
Walch Reproducible Books

Purchasers of this book are granted the right to reproduce all pages.

This permission is limited to a single teacher, for classroom use only.

Any questions regarding this policy or requests to purchase further reproduction rights should be addressed to

Permissions Editor
J. Weston Walch, Publisher
321 Valley Street • P.O. Box 658
Portland, Maine 04104-0658

1   2   3   4   5   6   7   8   9   10
ISBN 0-8251-4451-5

Copyright © 1994, 2002
J. Weston Walch, Publisher
P.O. Box 658 • Portland, Maine 04104-0658
www.walch.com

Printed in the United States of America

CONTENTS

Teacher Introduction

"It is like writing history with lightning!"

Woodrow Wilson exclaimed this in 1915, upon viewing D. W. Griffith's film *The Birth of a Nation*. Today, we are fairly blasé about films and television programs that have, or purport to have, themes based on historical subjects. Yet it is an accepted fact today that, for many people, these media are their only glimpse of history outside a formal classroom. For our students, films and television provide a chief source of entertainment and, sadly, in many cases the students totally accept what they see on the screen as absolute fact.

With this in mind, it is our purpose to present some sample films you can tie to a U.S. history curriculum and give you some ideas about using these films in the most productive way possible. We hope you can use these films in a broader context as a means of stimulating media awareness and critical-viewing skills in your students—turning "media-passive" students into "media-active" students who see the viewing of a film not as a comfortable break from classroom work but as a lesson in critical analysis and historical interpretation.

To do this, we must look at ways in which films can be used in a history classroom. Students are taught to analyze historical documents. A film can be analyzed and studied in much the same way. Several major questions could be asked of the film document: What is the content of the film? What information does it convey or portray? How is the information affected or determined by the necessity to entertain as well as instruct? What influences were at work during the production of the film—e.g., censorship, monetary constraints, attitudes of society, background of producers? How was the film received when it was released? This is not to say that films should not be enjoyed, but we must employ a bit of caution in the process. We must teach our students that in print and film, there is no such thing as a completely objective and unbiased historical account.

The films chosen for this book are presentations of history rather than documentations of history. That is, they are reenactments of historical events rather than documentary records of events, such as a newsreel or actuality footage. These historical-presentation films may present historical content in four ways:

1. **As a factual record:** It is possible to use film to dramatize what happened in the past. Some directors have taken great care to portray historical events accurately; Richard Attenborough's *A Bridge Too Far* (1977), Michael Mann's *The Insider* (1999), and Roger Donaldson's *Thirteen Days* (2000) are examples. Occasionally, historians act as advisers or even participate in the production of such films. A good example of this is the role Daniel J. Walkowitz played in the making of the television drama *Molders of Troy* (1979), which recreates the struggles of iron molders in upstate New York in the years 1859 to 1876.

2. **To convey atmosphere:** It is common for history teachers to use fiction to convey a sense of the past—lifestyles, values, or beliefs. Film-makers have spent much money, time, and energy to make historical presentations—whether fact-based, fictional, or docudramatic (combining elements of each)—look real. Costumes, sets, weapons, and props are often carefully reconstructed to lend legitimacy to

the production. Makers of fictional films like *Ragtime* (1981) take great care in creating an accurate setting (in this case, New York in 1906) for fictional events. Films loosely based on real characters or events, such as Barry Levinson's Baltimore stories, *Diner* (1982), *Tin Men* (1987), *Avalon* (1990), and *Liberty Heights* (1999); Woody Allen's *Radio Days* (1987); or Neil Simon's *Brighton Beach Memoirs* (1986), recreate with scrupulous honesty the look and sounds of the time period in which they are set. Makers of historical epics, such as James Cruze's *The Covered Wagon* (1923) and John Ford's *The Iron Horse* (1924), which used participants and their descendants as extras; John Wayne's *The Alamo* (1960), which recreated the San Antonio de Behar Mission, whatever the liberties it took with its historical characters; and *Glory* (1989), take great pains to create an accurate historical context for their stories.

3. **Analogy:** Occasionally, media producers use a historical event to point out or explain contemporary motives or actions, particularly when the contemporary event is controversial. *Sergeant York,* an idealized and partly fictional biographical film about an American World War I hero, was made in 1941 to convey a preparedness message to a country torn between interventionists and isolationists as World War II raged all around it. Similarly, many of President Woodrow Wilson's shortcomings in his handling of World War I peacemaking were glossed over in the 1944 biographical film called *Wilson* to present an interpretation designed to support Franklin Roosevelt's vision of a postwar United Nations. Ralph Nelson's graphic reenactment of the Sand Creek Massacre, *Soldier Blue* (1970), is transposed to the halfway point in the Indian Wars period of American history to draw a continuum between the army's attitude toward and treatment of Native Americans in the nineteenth century and its actions at My Lai (1970) in the then-ongoing Vietnam War. In much the

same way, many of the best science fiction films, from *2001: A Space Odyssey* to the original *Planet of the Apes,* both released in 1968, are meant as allegories, illuminating by analogy contemporary issues.

4. **As a lesson in historiography:** Because the dramatic form used in films required consistent and relatively simple motivational interpretations, students can often learn how the time period in which the film was made interpreted historical (and by implication contemporary) personalities or events. The narrow Freudianism that displayed the evils of society as the cause of deviant behavior during the early Cold War period can also be seen in contemporary dramas like *White Heat* (1949) and in such historical dramas as Gore Vidal's *The Left-Handed Gun* (1958), about Billy the Kid. *Dances with Wolves* (1990) demonstrated the growing awareness of the environment at the time the film was produced as well as a new appreciation for anything having to do with Native Americans.

Media resources have expanded dramatically in recent years, with new titles available every month. The films we have selected to key to U.S. history units are readily available in videocassette form, as well as, in some cases, digital videodisc (DVD). Many of our selected films are currently popular with U.S. history teachers. We also provide a list of other appropriate films for each unit. Since the distribution of videotapes and DVDs changes frequently, we have included a bibliography of media sources that you can use to check the availability of films. More and more films are becoming available on DVD, and this provides you with some advantages. Many DVDs contain ancillary materials on the film such as outtakes, newsreel footage from the time period of the film, or interviews with historical consultants. When a DVD player is interfaced with a computer, often there are hot links that can be used to go directly to web sites on related topics. If a computer interface is not possible, you can copy down the uniform resource locators (URLs) from the DVD and use them on a separate computer to research web sites. As the technology changes, films and other video resources are becoming easier and easier for teachers to use. Freezing an image, rewinding, and replaying a section of a film is much simpler than it has been in the past.

Reproducible student material contained in this book includes A Student Introduction to Historical Films (page *x*), a Film Analysis Guide Sheet (page 143), and a Glossary of Common Film Terms (page 146) to aid in film analysis. Most units also include reproducible student pages consisting of a guide to what to watch for in a film and a worksheet that includes a vocabulary list and questions based on the film. We suggest that you hand out both the Film Analysis Guide Sheet and the unit's reproducible pages to students before they view the particular film. The vocabulary lists refer specifically to terms used in the film or in the introductory materials provided in the unit. The terms can be reviewed by you with the students before they watch the film or can be defined by the students as part of their written assignment or during class discussion. Likewise, you can decide how to use the worksheet questions—as a written assignment, a springboard for class discussion, or an enrichment assignment to be completed at home.

You will find that Unit 16 is different from the previous units in that it provides a case study on how a historical event—the OK Corral gunfight in this instance—has been redefined by filmmakers immersed in responding to, or wishing to profit from, popular attitudes or beliefs that existed when each of the films was made. This unit analyzes three of the many film versions of the gunfight. The first, *My Darling Clementine,* was made just after World War II as the victorious Allies, including the United States and Soviet Union, were justifying their own participation in the war in the light of rising Cold War tensions. The second, *Gunfight at the OK Corral,* appeared at the midpoint of the Eisenhower administration when Americans were acting abroad as the globe's police force, ferreting out Communists even if that meant supporting corrupt dictators while uncovering organized crime at home and enjoying the material rewards

of "melting pot" conformity. The third, *Doc,* was produced at the height of the disillusionment and polarization resulting from the Vietnam War, which was manifested in the antiwar, counterculture, and minority-empowerment movements. The unit is written primarily for your own enrichment and to suggest additional ways in which use of films can illuminate the study of U.S. history and its interpretive shifts. But these examples might also be used productively with a more advanced American history class, especially since (given the limited class time available) the first two films are widely available on videocassettes and DVDs and can be watched by students outside of class. A reproducible student question sheet has been provided for use with each individual film in the unit as well as a question that asks students to compare the disparate views of all three films on this event.

Finally, we also need to remind our students that movies are produced primarily as vehicles for entertainment. Actors and actresses are generally chosen because they are attractive to the audience. Their characters may have fought in a battle, but their hair is usually clean and their teeth are sparkling white. In their film of seventeenth century England, *Winstanley* (1975), directors Kevin Brownlow and Andrew Mollo sought to present an accurate image of life at that time. The directors hired nonprofessional actors with careworn faces, matted hair, and bad teeth. Costumes were worn for the duration of the shooting without being laundered and cast members did not engage in modern hygiene. The comment from most students in viewing this film is "Yuck!" It is important to explain to students that life in the past was not as clean, manicured, and beautifully coiffured as is usually portrayed by Hollywood.

We hope that you will find ways to use film as a positive teaching tool, providing an active viewing experience for your class. In our role as social studies teachers, we now need to add critical-viewing skills (or visual literacy) to the list of important abilities our students need to develop for life in our media-conscious society.

A Layperson's Note on Copyright and Fair Use

Copyright is a delicate balancing effort undertaken by the federal government, on the one hand, to encourage intellectual and artistic creativity by ensuring a fair return for the artist's efforts (as well as profit-engendered distribution systems) while, on the other, to provide an environment in which these ideas and achievements can spread widely to be judged in public review and analysis. Educators have long relied on the doctrine of "fair use" to permit copyrighted materials to be used in their classrooms without prior authorization. The Copyright Law of 1976 substantially circumscribed the concept of fair use, while the results of the author-user conference that accompanied the law's development suggested specific guidelines of brevity, spontaneity, and "cumulative effect"—that is, the extent to which the use interferes with the author's potential market—to help determine whether projected use of copyrighted material is permissible under the law. Both because this was a compromise between users and authors, and because the law attempted to encompass the range of print and electronic media invented since the 1905 law, these guidelines were necessarily vague. Subsequent amendments and additions to the law, such as the Digital Millennium Copyright Act of 1998 and the Sonny Bono Copyright Term Extension Act of 1998, have done little to lend clarity to the situation. The new nonprint media have been an area of particular contention between authors and users, partly because of their ephemeral nature and ease of broadcasting and partly because of the threat posed to producers and distributors by the explosion in the availability and ease of duplication technologies.

The law in this area is still developing, and definitive conclusions are not yet possible. When films, tapes, or discs are purchased or rented from legitimate educational distributors, specific use licenses accompany them. Beyond this, it is probably legal to use other commercial tapes legitimately acquired by purchase, rental, or lease in direct face-to-face instruction. It is likely not legal to broadcast them over closed-circuit, instructional, or broadcast radio or television systems or to digitize and send them over the Web without a specific license to do so. It is probably illegal to deposit them in libraries for casual listening or viewing, to play them publicly to general (even student) or paying audiences, or to use pirated tapes for these purposes. Copies made without permission from other tapes, films, or other recordings are, except for limited preservation purposes, considered pirated copies, even if the recordings from which they were obtained are legitimate.

Under certain circumstances, downloaded or "off-air" copies may also be legally employed in this same face-to-face instruction for a very limited time before they must be erased, though these should probably be recorded at the site of their proposed "time-shifted" use. ("Off-air" recording means the recording of a televised program, such as a PBS documentary. "Time-shifted" use is the showing of a recorded videotape at a time to suit an individual's need, such as conforming to a specific class meeting time.) To facilitate such use, many educational distributors are offering to license such recordings for educational purposes for a set time or for the life of the tape as an alternative to more expensive rentals or purchases. In addition, specialized off-air and commercial copy-licensing clearinghouses are now in existence or are being formed.

The legitimacy of excerpting unauthorized clips or cuts for summary presentation, review, or critical analysis remains an open question (those seen or heard on television or radio previews or review programs are provided by the distributors for this use). Many areas of nonprint media use remain murky or undefined.

With respect to web-based material, the law regarding electronic media and fair use is still in its early stages of development and subject to continuing dispute and litigation. In light of this, if you are not certain of the public domain or free-use status of such electronic material, seek permission for any computer-based use beyond their live display via hot links. If doubts remain (either with respect to the material itself or the wording of the permission you obtain) and you want your electronic presentations to display material from other web sites, it is safest for you to hot link to those sites, rather than download scenes from them. If you want your students to have access to or to review such materials, provide them with the URLs for the sites on which the material is found so that they can get access to the materials themselves.

In all of these areas, it is important to consult some of the many guides available from professional organizations, clearinghouses, or copyright experts and to seek legal advice (often available at the district level or through the local superintendent's office) where the fact or situation of the proposed media use raises questions or poses special problems.

A Student Introduction to Historical Films

You have probably heard the expressions "Seeing is believing" and "A picture is worth a thousand words." It may seem to you that a truthful and enjoyable way to learn history is through pictures—moving pictures, or films. It is true that films do provide us with presentations of historical events, such as the Vietnam War or the French Revolution. Historical themes have been popular as long as motion pictures have been produced. It is also true, however, that films provide us with *interpretations* of historical figures and events. Just as you have learned to be critical of print documents, you must bring a critical eye to nonprint or media documents. It is important to use critical-viewing skills when you see media productions in your social studies classes, on television at home, or at the movies.

In order to use films to their full advantage, ask several major questions when viewing a film:

1. What is the content of the film? What information does it convey?

2. How and/or why was the film produced? What forces were at work during its production that might have affected its final form? (For example: Censorship? Background of the producers? Budgetary limitations?)

3. How was the film received when it came out? Was it popular? Did it have any effect on the attitudes of the people who saw it?

Since films are produced first of all to entertain and, perhaps, secondly to instruct, it is important to remember that few film producers are willing to risk the box office draw of their film for historical accuracy. If a choice must be made between entertainment and historical fact, the truth might suffer. If this is so, why use a film for learning at all? Why not use all print materials such as textbooks and readings?

First, print materials, like films, involve interpretation and careful analysis to determine historical fact. Films can also be a valuable way of going back through time to experience the atmosphere of a past era or to "see" historical characters long

(continued)

dead. Many film production companies try very hard to make the settings for their historical presentation as accurate as possible. They employ historians as consultants to advise in the construction of sets, costume design, weaponry, transportation, manners, and other details. Sometimes historians play an even more central role. A good example of this is the film *Denmark Vesey's Rebellion* (1981). Noted American historian Robert B. Toplin acted as the project director for the film and was assisted by a scholarly panel. They were to ensure not only the accuracy of the visual details (the film was shot at various Southern locations including historic Charleston), but also, and more importantly, the faithfulness of the historical interpretation of what historians understand actually happened. Toplin participated in every stage of the production, ensuring that the film of this 1822 slave rebellion would avoid stereotyping its characters or reduce complex and controversial events to a conventional Hollywood plot line. The resulting film, starring Yaphet Kotto, Ned Beatty, and Cleavon Little, was broadcast on the Public Broadcasting System as part of the *A House Divided* series, and it won numerous awards.

Other films are less true to history and are designed primarily for entertainment with little regard for fact. The best example of this is the Academy Award-winning movie *Braveheart* (1995). William Wallace was a real person who lived between 1272–1305 in Scotland. And he did lead the Scottish war for independence from England. Other than the rather grisly method of his execution, little else in this film is historically true. The real Wallace was a knight who wore battle armor and never would have worn a kilt. He lived in a substantial house and not an earthen mound. Was this a good film? Certainly it was very entertaining and inspiring. When shown in Scotland, it caused the audiences to jump to their feet and join the actors in shouting "Freedom! Freedom!" Membership in the Scottish National Party or SNP rose dramatically after *Braveheart* finished its run in the Scottish movie theaters. It is an exciting and well acted film, and it has entertainment value, but it is not accurate history, nor was it probably meant to be.

When you watch films in class, complete assignments, and have class discussions, try to keep in mind what the purpose of a film is—primarily entertainment. Also, try to see in what ways the films provide a greater lesson in historical interpretation and critical analysis. Above all, enjoy the unique experience of actively evaluating and analyzing a film document rather than being a passive receiver of its message.

The Colonial Experience

TEACHER'S GUIDE

THREE SOVEREIGNS FOR SARAH

Nightowl Productions, 1986; directed by Philip Leacock, color, 172 minutes

BACKGROUND OF THE FILM

This three-episode video was originally presented on public television. It is based on extensive research into the period of the Salem witch trials, notably the book *Salem Possessed: The Social Origins of Witchcraft,* by Paul Boyer and Stephen Nissenbaum. The outbreak of hysteria in Salem, Massachusetts, in 1692, which resulted in the execution of 19 people as witches, has been the subject of many books, stories, and plays such as *The Crucible* by Arthur Miller. This film looks at this event as part of a series of social and political disputes that occurred in Salem.

As early as 1700, Robert Calef wrote an analysis of the witch trials in Salem Village (now Danvers, Massachusetts) that pointed to the serious social divisions in the village itself and the opposition felt by many villagers against the more worldly and affluent port, Salem Town. The inland Salem Village was far more rural, and it was subordinate to the influences of Salem Town. In 1689, Salem Village chose a new minister, and this engendered a division within the village itself. The man ultimately selected was Reverend Samuel Parris, a failed merchant who had never held a position in a church. A dispute between pro-Parris and anti-Parris factions left deep scars in the village community. Parris's most outspoken supporter was Thomas Putnam. Very vocal in his opposition to Parris was Joseph Putnam, Thomas's stepbrother, who had inherited their father's wealth.

The film uses this rivalry as a focal point, again based on the research by Boyer, Nissenbaum, and others.

The theory presented is that the "afflicted" children began their accusations as a game. The adults then used the girls' afflictions and accusations as a way to get back at their enemies, especially those who had opposed Parris. Thomas Putnam's wife, Ann, was particularly instrumental in the accusations. She sought to avenge herself over the loss of her husband's inheritance as well as losses in her own family. Ann Putnam's family had lost land and status to a family of three sisters, Rebecca Nurse, Mary Easty, and Sarah Cloyce. The movie presents these village divisions through the narration of the surviving sister, Sarah Cloyce, as she strives to clear her sisters' names.

The film's dialogue is based on original transcripts of the trial and Sarah's diary. The costumes, buildings, locations, and props attempt to be faithful to the late 1600s in America. Many of the original locations were used in Salem, Danvers, and Ipswich, Massachusetts. The script also gives a good glimpse of the fundamental religious nature of life in Puritan Massachusetts.

SYNOPSIS OF THE PLOT

Since it was made to be a television series, this film is in three episodes. Episode One begins in Boston in 1703. A woman in ill health, Sarah Cloyce, has come with her nephew, Samuel Nurse, to testify before magistrates at a private hearing. Sarah wishes to clear her sisters' names from the charge of witchcraft. She tells the judges a story of conspiracy and family rivalry in Salem Village, which were the factors that led to the accusations of witchcraft.

In a flashback, the story returns to June 1689, when Salem Village was picking a new minister for its meetinghouse. Thomas Putnam wants Reverend Samuel Parris. He is opposed by his stepbrother, Joseph Putnam, one of the wealthiest village landholders. In November of 1689, Parris does become minister. He preaches his first sermon, in which he equates his supporters with holiness. In February 1692, Parris's daughter Betty, his niece Abigail Williams, and Ann Putnam, Jr., begin to have fits after practicing crystal reading with Tituba, Parris's West Indian slave. When a doctor is sent for, he proclaims that the children are bewitched. The children are finally brought together in Thomas Putnam's house, and they name Tituba and two other women as witches.

During her testimony in 1703, Sarah explains to the judges how these girls were influenced by their guardians. The names came from adults such as Ann Putnam, rather than from the children themselves.

Back again in 1692, Sarah is visiting her ailing sister, Rebecca Nurse. She is joined by her other sister, Mary Easty. Rebecca's son, Samuel, and Joseph Putnam arrive to tell Rebecca that she is to be arrested for witchcraft.

Episode Two begins in March 1692, with an examination held in the Salem Village meetinghouse. The girls and Ann Putnam accuse Rebecca of being a witch. When the girls have fits, Rebecca is sent to trial for witchcraft along with Sarah Good, another woman of Salem Village.

When Samuel Parris preaches an inflammatory sermon, Sarah stands up and leaves, slamming the door behind her. The children then have fits and name Sarah as their tormentor. Sarah is later arrested. She is stripped and searched for devil's marks. She is then brought before the magistrate to be examined. The children once more have hysterical fits and name Sarah as a witch. Sarah is taken to prison to await trial.

As Joseph and Samuel ride to find help, they pass an elderly man, Giles Corey, being pressed to death for refusing to plead either guilty or innocent of being a wizard.

In prison Sarah meets Tituba, who has confessed to being a witch. Tituba shows Sarah the wounds she has from being beaten until she confessed. More and more of the accused are filling the prison. As the episode ends, Mary Easty is arrested for witchcraft.

Episode Three begins with Mary Easty being acquitted for lack of evidence. She is rearrested, though, and thrown into prison when another child names her. The evidence used is "spectral evidence"— the claim that Mary's specter has been tormenting the child, the most difficult charge for defendants to deny. Rebecca Nurse is found guilty and sentenced to death. She is brought before her minister, Nicholas Noyes, and excommunicated. On July 19, 1692, Sarah Good and Rebecca Nurse are hanged.

Mary Easty is next brought to trial and found guilty. As time goes on, surrounding towns borrow the afflicted girls to point out witches in their communities. Despite the power of the girls, Parris's influence erodes and he loses his salary. On September 22, many more accused witches are hanged, not just from Salem but other towns as well. Mary Easty is executed.

Sarah is taken from prison in Salem to a private jail to relieve overcrowding. Her health deteriorates in the poor conditions of her confinement. Finally, Samuel and Peter Cloyce come to free Sarah; the governor has issued a general pardon to all those accused. Ministers above Parris have rejected spectral evidence as proof of witchcraft.

The program moves forward again to 1703. Sarah presents evidence of a conspiracy to the magistrates. The judges state that while years may pass before any final judgment will be made on the accused, she and her sisters are absolved from wrong. They give Sarah three gold sovereigns as a symbol, one for each of the three sisters wrongly accused of witchcraft. The story ends with Sarah telling what happened to the primary accusers after the witch trials. Mary's and Rebecca's names were completely cleared in 1711, and in 1712 Rebecca's excommunication was overturned. Sarah Cloyce died three weeks after the hearings and was buried with the three gold sovereigns.

IDEAS FOR CLASS DISCUSSION

The American colonies saw one of the last major outbursts of witchcraft hysteria in the civilized world. A good focus for class discussion might be to discern why this was so. Was Europe so far ahead intellectually due to the Scientific Revolution? Did the upheaval caused by the rise of the new scientific view of the world encourage a search for scapegoats? Or was there something inherent in American Puritanism that could account for this? *The Crucible* by Arthur Miller would be an appropriate reading to accompany the viewing of this film. In writing his play Miller was protesting the witch trial-like hysteria of the McCarthy era. Perhaps the social, economic, and political background of events in Salem Village can account for the witchcraft trials, as suggested by Boyer and Nissenbaum in their book, just as McCarthy's outbursts were influenced by the political events of his day. Is the desire for human gain or the desire to find someone to blame for unsettling change the unifying force in both cases?

BOOKS AND MATERIALS RELATING TO THIS FILM AND TOPIC

Boyer, Paul S., and Stephen Nissenbaum. *Salem Possessed: The Social Origins of Witchcraft.* Cambridge, MA: Harvard University Press, 1974.

Karlsen, Carol F. *The Devil in the Shape of a Woman: Witchcraft in Colonial New England.* New York: W. W. Norton, 1987.

Weisman, Richard. *Witchcraft, Magic, and Religion in 17th Century Massachusetts.* Amherst: University of Massachusetts Press, 1984.

Zeinert, Karen. *The Salem Witchcraft Trials.* New York: Franklin Watts, 1989.

OTHER MEDIA RESOURCES FOR THIS TIME PERIOD

The Crucible (1996, 123 minutes) Daniel Day-Lewis and Winona Ryder star in this Arthur Miller screenplay set in Salem, Massachusetts, in 1692; it is a parable of Senator Joseph McCarthy's Communist witchhunts of the 1950s.

The Last of the Mohicans (1992, 114 minutes) Retells James Fenimore Cooper's frontier story, replacing the racism of the original with a careful recreation of European–Native American relations at the time of the French and Indian War; the film is rated **R** because the violence of that conflict is realistically portrayed.

Mayflower (1970, 90 minutes) A made-for-television movie with Anthony Hopkins as the ship captain and Richard Crenna as William Brewster, this film tells about the Pilgrims' decision to emigrate and the voyage to the New World.

Plymouth Aventure (1952, 102 minutes) This film deals with the founding of the Massachusetts colony.

Roanoke (1986, 180 minutes) A three-part, made-for-television movie about the early contacts between English explorers and settlers and the Algonquian-speaking native population along the North American coast of what is now North Carolina; the story is told through the relationship between the Roanoke governor and artist John White and two native warriors, Wanchese and Manteo.

The Scarlet Letter (1972, 94 minutes) Based on Hawthorne's classic tale of adultery in seventeenth-century Salem, Massachusetts

Squanto: A Warrior's Tale (1994, 102 minutes) The story of the Native American who befriended the Pilgrim settlers

THREE SOVEREIGNS FOR SARAH

Nightowl Productions, 1986; directed by Philip Leacock

Major Character	Actor/Actress
Sarah Cloyce	Vanessa Redgrave
Samuel Nurse	Ronald Hunter
Reverend Samuel Parris	Will Lyman
Rebecca Nurse	Phyllis Thaxter
Mary Easty	Kim Hunter
Chief magistrate	Patrick McGoohan
Joseph Putnam	John Dukakis
Thomas Putnam	Daniel von Bargen
Ann Putnam, Sr.	Maryann Plunkett

WHAT TO WATCH FOR

This made-for-TV movie deals with an episode in American history that is both fascinating and repellent to many—the Salem witch trials of 1692. The film captures accurately the events of the time using the manuscripts of the trials and Sarah Cloyce's diary for dialogue. It also gives us a glimpse of historical detective work into the past to uncover why these witchhunts may have started. The hysterical accusations of witchcraft, which pitted neighbor against neighbor in Salem Village (now Danvers), Massachusetts, has been a subject of investigation and hypothesis for three hundred years. Two historians, Paul Boyer and Stephen Nissenbaum, believe that they have successfully explained the reason for the start of these witchcraft accusations and for such widespread acceptance of the claims that caused hundreds of people to be accused of being witches.

(continued)

Boyer and Nissenbaum's well accepted theory is that there was a division in Salem Village in the 1690s that pitted its less well-to-do people against their neighbors in the nearby and affluent Salem Town. The supporters of the controversial minister of Salem Village, Reverend Samuel Parris, particularly Ann Putnam, had personal and family grievances over land and inheritance against many of the accused who did not support Parris. The main character, Sarah Cloyce, sets out this theory in order to exonerate her two older sisters, Rebecca Nurse and Mary Easty, who were hanged for practicing witchcraft.

Note the costumes, props, buildings, and settings. These are accurate recreations of seventeenth-century New England. Note also the importance of religion in this Puritan community. An interesting comparison could be made between our court system today and justice as it was practiced in 1692.

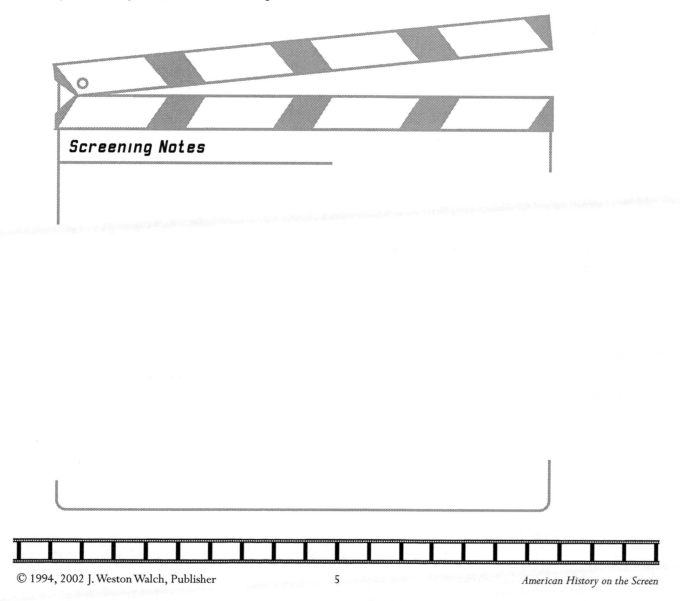

Screening Notes

— *THREE SOVEREIGNS FOR SARAH* —————————————————

VOCABULARY

excommunication   restitution

magistrate   specter

meetinghouse   witchcraft

Puritan

QUESTIONS BASED ON THE FILM

1. What happened in England in 1688 that has affected the colonies and caused them,
   in Sarah's words, to "feel adrift"?

   _____

   _____

   _____

2. What economic and cultural differences are there between Salem Village and
   Salem Town?

   _____

   _____

   _____

3. Why does Ann Putnam have grievances against Sarah Cloyce's family?

   _____

   _____

   _____

(continued)

4. According to Sarah, why is Rebecca accused of witchcraft?

_____

_____

_____

5. What are the tests for sorcery that are used at Sarah's trial? _____

_____

_____

6. Why does Tituba confess to being a witch? _____

_____

_____

7. Why is the sentence of excommunication the worst punishment for Rebecca Nurse?

_____

_____

_____

8. Why do the witchhunts finally stop? _____

_____

_____

9. What evidence of a conspiracy does Sarah present to the magistrates at Boston in 1703?

_____

_____

_____

The American Revolution

TEACHER'S GUIDE

THE PATRIOT

Columbia Pictures Corporation, 2000; directed by Roland Emmerich, color, 157 minutes

Note: This film is rated **R** due to the violence of the battle scenes, but is contained in many educational video catalogs. You may wish to use a parental permission form.

BACKGROUND OF THE FILM

For such a formative period in our nation's history, the American Revolution is featured in many fewer films than the western expansion of America or the Vietnam War. *The Patriot* is a film with all of the elements of a commercially viable Hollywood movie: adventure, drama, color, romance, and a "good triumphs over evil" ending. It is also a film for which considerable effort was made to place the story within a historically accurate frame. To achieve this end, the production staff engaged several departments of the Smithsonian Institution's National Museum of American History to advise them on such things as uniforms, weapons, battle formations, furniture, and the many aspects of eighteenth-century American life portrayed in the film.

Recommendations from Smithsonian personnel often took the story in new directions. For example, the chairman of the museum's cultural division suggested that a good hiding place for the Martin family could have been a maroon village. There were many of these hidden communities established by runaway slaves; they were held together by the Gullah language, a patois of native West African languages and English. Maroon villages usually were not located on the water, as shown in the film, but deep in the woods and swamps. The coastal location was chosen by filmmakers for its esthetic look—one of a few compromises made between historical accuracy and visual appeal.

The costumes, weapons, and battle tactics were carefully researched. Actors had to learn to load and fire the six-foot-long muskets. (In fact, because of the long reloading intervals and relative inaccuracy of these weapons, the authentic eighteenth-century military tactic of lining armies up to face each other was not quite as suicidal as it appears today.) Contemporary reenactors were used as extras to portray colonial-era soldiers; they were then multiplied by computer-generated special effects. The scenes in which cannon balls roll or bounce into a line is based on fact. Cannon balls did not explode upon impact, as is the common misconception; they killed people by the force of contact, causing the loss of body parts. Chain shot was used to wipe out larger numbers of an advancing line of soldiers. One costume change made by the filmmakers was to have the British Green Dragoons wear mostly red coats instead of green; this was to make it clear to the audience that these men were on the British side.

Students will doubtless want to know about the bundling bag that Gabriel is sewn into in order to spend the night with Anne without any impropriety. This was true to the time period. In colder climates, couples courted in the warmth of a bed with a bundling board separating them.

The main characters in the film, with the exception of Lord Cornwallis, are not real historical figures, but they are very often based upon real people or composites of several people. Mel Gibson's character is a composite of several Revolutionary War heroes who used unconventional (later called "guerilla") tactics against the better armed and trained British, who regarded them as operating beyond the pale of civilized warfare. The models for Gibson's character include Francis Marion, Thomas Sumter, Daniel Morgan, Andrew Pickens, and Elijah Clark. Marion, known as the Swamp Fox, had his own militia and used surprise tactics against the British much as the Ghost does in this film. The chief villain, Colonel Tavington, is based upon Lieutenant Banastre Tarleton. Tarleton was known for his cruelty in having Americans killed even after they had put down their arms and surrendered. However, the extreme brutality shown to the civilian population in the film was not practiced by Tarleton, although he was generally known as the Butcher. This misrepresentation caused a good deal of criticism in the British press when the film was released in the United Kingdom.

Another inaccuracy in the movie is that slaves were *not* automatically granted their freedom by either the British or the Continental army if they fought. Some slaves did serve in their masters' places and could be granted freedom for this deed, but most slaves who fought actually returned to bondage. Yet, the American Revolution did see the last integrated army until the Korean War. According to the filmmakers, the last scene of the movie is symbolic as Martin arrives to find the former bigot and the former slave working together to rebuild his house. The underlying mission of the American Revolution was the building of freedom for all people—a task which some might argue has still not been completed even today.

SYNOPSIS OF THE PLOT

The hero of this film is Benjamin Martin, a widower with six children who lives on his farm in South Carolina. A veteran of the French and Indian War, Benjamin feels guilty about his role in that conflict and does not wish to join the revolution as either a Loyalist or a Rebel. The film opens in 1776, with a post rider arriving at the Martin's farm with mail. An assembly has been called in Charles Town (now known as Charleston); as a result, the entire Martin family goes to the city. Benjamin attends the assembly, but he declares that he will not fight, despite encouragement from his former comrade Harry Burwell, who is serving as a Rebel officer. South Carolina votes to join the war; Benjamin's oldest son, Gabriel, enlists in the Continental Army.

Back at the farm some time later, a letter arrives from Gabriel. He writes that things are going badly for the colonial regulars. As the family eats dinner, Gabriel actually staggers in, wounded from a local battle between the British Green Dragoons and the Virginia Regulars. As Benjamin watches, a battle rages just outside; he takes in the wounded from both sides.

The leader of the Green Dragoons, Colonel Tavington, orders the Martins' house and barn to be burned. He captures Gabriel to have him hanged and orders that the Rebel wounded be killed. When Benjamin's 15-year-old son, Thomas, tries to save his brother, Tavington shoots and kills him. Then, as the house burns, Benjamin rushes in and gathers up his weapons from the French and Indian War. He and his two younger sons hide in the woods, ambush the British troops, and rescue Gabriel. Benjamin slaughters a British soldier with a tomahawk in a wild frenzy of anger and grief. At the British camp, a survivor tells Tavington that the slaughter has been the work of just one man, and at this point Benjamin is labeled the Ghost.

Benjamin takes his family to Aunt Charlotte's (his sister-in-law's) plantation. Gabriel goes off to rejoin the army; Benjamin then decides to go after him. They watch from an abandoned house as the colonial army under General Gates is soundly defeated by the British regulars at the Battle of Camden (August 1780). Benjamin meets with the only officer left on the American side, Colonel Harry Burwell, and tells him the cause is lost unless the Rebels stop trying to confront the British in the conventional European manner. They must keep General Cornwallis from moving north until the French can arrive with reinforcements. Benjamin meets Major Jean Villeneuve, a Frenchman fighting with the Americans (the French recognized the American insurgents in 1777, after the American success at Saratoga). Benjamin is made a colonel and is allowed to form his own militia.

At Cornwallis's headquarters, the general receives a land grant from King George in return for his service. He orders Tavington to stop his brutal tactics and to fight like a gentleman.

Gabriel and Benjamin go off to find men to enlist in the militia. At the village of Pembroke, Gabriel goes into a church and asks men to join the cause. A young woman, Anne Howard, stands up and encourages the men in the congregation to enlist. Gabriel asks Anne's father if he can write to her. Benjamin goes to a tavern and finds many of his former fellow soldiers from the French and Indian War—now farmers and rough-hewn frontiersmen. One man is too ill to fight, but he sends his slave, Occam, to fight for him. Although Gabriel feels that these men are not the right sort to fight a gentleman's war, Benjamin disagrees. The militia men ambush the British time and time again, even capturing baggage, personal correspondence, and dogs belonging to General Cornwallis. At a ball in Charleston, Cornwallis is angered over the stories about the Ghost; he becomes even angrier when his supply ship is blown up.

When the militia block a road and attempt to capture some British wagons, they fall into a trap. Many are killed and wounded. Occam arrives back at the camp to warn Benjamin that the British are going to begin hanging the captured Rebels one at a time until the Ghost gives himself up. Benjamin goes to the headquarters of Cornwallis under a white flag to negotiate a prisoner exchange. Cornwallis argues that officers should not be targeted in warfare, but Benjamin states that as long as civilians are killed, officers will be targeted. Tavington taunts Benjamin about Thomas's death; Benjamin says that before the war is over, he will kill Tavington. The captured militia members are released, but Cornwallis then learns that the British officers who have supposedly been held by Benjamin are actually straw-filled effigies and that he has been tricked. Tavington tells Cornwallis that the only way to capture Benjamin and the militia is with brutal tactics. He finds out through the Martins' neighbor, who has sided with the British, who the Ghost is and where his family is probably hidden.

Tavington goes to Charlotte's Charles Town plantation to find Benjamin's children. Charlotte hides the children in the cellar, and Gabriel then arrives to take them to a Gullah maroon village where they will be safe.

At the camp, Benjamin finds out that Tavington has a list of the men in the militia and that he is burning their homes. When John Billings, one of Benjamin's most trusted men, finds his wife and child killed, he shoots himself in the head. Benjamin gives his men a week-long furlough to tend to their families; he heads for the Gullah village. Anne Howard and her family arrive at the village, and she and Gabriel are married. When Benjamin and Gabriel return to their camp, they fear that no one will return. One by one, however, the men show up.

At the village of Pembroke, Tavington and his soldiers arrive. They lock the inhabitants in the church and burn it, killing all inside, including Anne and her family. Martin and the militia arrive to find the town destroyed. Gabriel leaves to seek revenge. He meets up with Tavington and is killed while fighting him.

Benjamin finds Gabriel as he is dying. He brings his body to the camp of the colonial regular army. Colonel Burwell begs Benjamin to join the army, but Benjamin refuses; he feels that his past sins in warfare have caught up with him. Later, though, when Benjamin finds an American flag that Gabriel has mended, he changes his mind. He rides to join the army, carrying the flag as his men cheer.

General Green is concerned about the reliability of the militia, but Benjamin convinces him to allow them to take the first two shots against the British regulars. As the battle begins, Cornwallis is amazed that the militia is at the center of the line. Tavington begins the charge without waiting for the order. The militia lead the British into an ambush by the Rebel army, and Tavington and Benjamin end up in hand-to-hand fighting. Benjamin kills Tavington after a long fight scene which required numerous changes of costume (note the continuity errors) for the main actors. This battle, modeled on the Battle of Cowpens, results in an American victory; Cornwallis orders a retreat.

The movie ends with a letter from Benjamin to Charlotte telling her that a French fleet has arrived with reinforcements and that Cornwallis has surrendered. Benjamin and Jean Villeneuve part as friends despite their earlier animosity. Charlotte and Benjamin return to his farm with his remaining children, to find his comrades from the militia rebuilding his house.

IDEAS FOR CLASS DISCUSSION

As is so often the case with Hollywood movies, the time line of the action in this film is compressed, appearing to take place over a matter of months instead of from 1776 to 1781, when Cornwallis surrendered at Yorktown. Students need to be reminded of this; the war was a long one, with many phases and twists and turns.

The war also caused divisions among the North American colonies; not everyone supported the Rebel cause. Many, like Benjamin's neighbor, sided with the British. Most of the Green Dragoons were American Loyalists, also known as Tories. At the end of the Revolutionary War, many of these Loyalists fled (or were dispossessed and forced to flee) to Canada, the Northwest Territories, or the Caribbean region. Who really were the "patriots"? Obviously, many Americans viewed this differently than the British did (and still do!).

The role of the French in the Revolutionary War is a good discussion topic. Throughout the film, Benjamin and Jean Villeneuve display animosity toward each other; it has not been long since the

French and Indian War, where the colonists fought alongside the British against the French. It has been stated that the Revolutionary War started in the North, was fought in the South, and was won by the French. Is this an accurate statement? Americans tend to think that colonial Americans won the war single-handedly, but French aid—sent more to humilitate the British than to support the Rebels— was indispensable.

This film certainly lends itself to a discussion about the balance between trying to "get it right" historically and selling a product of entertainment, especially since the filmmakers' collaboration with the Smithsonian is so well documented. Are compromises acceptable, such as the use of the American flag in the battle scenes, when experts do not agree about what form the flag actually took or even whether it would have been used? Are the atrocities committed by the British Dragoons essential to show, or do they pander to our darker instincts—our desire for purely evil villains to justify the hero's extreme acts, the blood and gore, and incessant action?

BOOKS AND MATERIALS RELATING TO THIS FILM AND TOPIC

"Capturing America's Fight for Freedom," *Smithsonian* 31, no. 4 (July 2000): 44–53.

Fritz, Suzanne and Rachel Aberly. *The Patriot: The Official Companion*. London: Carlton Books, 2000.

Kaplan, Sidney, and Emma Nogrady Kaplan. *The Black Presence in the Era of the American Revolution*. Amherst: University of Massachusetts Press, 1989.

OTHER MEDIA RESOURCES FOR THIS TIME PERIOD

America (1924, 95 minutes) D.W. Griffith's silent-era epic of the war; its battle scenes, tableaus of famous events, and period recreations still hold up quite well, although a saccharine love story mars the overall effect.

The Crossing (2000, 90 minutes) An A&E recreation starring Jeff Daniels as George Washington;

Howard Fast, who wrote a novel about the crossing of the Delaware, wrote the screenplay.

Drums Along the Mohawk (1939, 103 minutes) Directed by John Ford, this film takes place in the Mohawk Valley, where Indian tribes loyal to the British posed a threat to settlers during the Revolution.

The Howards of Virginia (1940, 122 minutes) Stars Cary Grant as a land surveyor who gets caught up in the Revolution

Jefferson in Paris (1995, 136 minutes) Before he was president, Thomas Jefferson was the American ambassador to France. This film looks at this part of Jefferson's life and speculates about his relationship with his slave Sally Hemmings.

Johnny Tremain (1957, 80 minutes) This film recreates the Boston Tea Party, Paul Revere's ride, and the battles at Lexington and Concord.

Revolution (1985, 125 minutes) An expensively made movie, but a bomb at the box office, this film culminates at the Battle of Yorktown.

Sally Hemmings: An American Scandal (2000, 173 minutes) A soap-operalike film about Jefferson's relationship with his slave

1776 (1972, 148 minutes) Based upon the musical play of the same name, this film is a recreation of the days from March through July 1776, when the Second Continental Congress wrestled with the idea of independence from England, culminating in the adoption of the Declaration of Independence.

THE PATRIOT

Columbia Pictures Corporation, 2000; directed by Ron Emmerich

Major Character	Actor/Actress
Benjamin Martin	Mel Gibson
Gabriel Martin	Heath Ledger
Colonel Tavington	Jason Isaacs
Lord General Cornwallis	Tom Wilkinson
Charlotte Selton	Joely Richardson
Anne Howard	Lisa Brenner
Major Jean Villeneuve	Tcheky Karyo
Colonel Harry Burwell	Chris Cooper

WHAT TO WATCH FOR

The making of this film was an unusual experience in Hollywood, as the production company collaborated with the Smithsonian Institution's National Museum of American History on the costumes, weapons, military tactics, household articles, and much more. Actors were trained to shoot the colonial-era reproduction weapons, and Mel Gibson spent many hours practicing hand-to-hand combat. Authentic uniforms were either made or rented, and sets like the Gullah maroon village were carefully constructed, with the houses made out of wattle-and-daub construction common to that time period. Despite this collaboration, however, some compromises were made—such as the uniforms of the Green Dragoons, which were changed to mostly red in order to identify them clearly as fighting on the British side.

Note the tactics of eighteenth-century warfare, which are accurately portrayed in the film. Each army basically lined up and faced each other while firing and marching

(continued)

forward. While some film critics have denounced the amount of bloodshed shown in the movie, this was probably the norm for battles of this type.

Many of the main characters are based on real people in history. Colonel Tavington of the Green Dragoons is based upon Lieutenant Banastre Tavington, who was known as the Butcher for his orders to kill any American troops who surrendered, even if they had put down their arms. Benjamin Martin is a composite of several Revolutionary-era heroes.

Note the animosity between Martin and Major Jean Villeneuve, a French officer serving in the militia. French aid was instrumental in winning this war, although American national pride tends to downplay the role of the French and emphasize national heroes like George Washington and Francis Marion.

Slaves who fought on either side in the Revolution were not guaranteed freedom after the war was over. Some slaves fought in place of their masters and were sometimes granted freedom for this, but the issue of freedom and liberty for all was not fully resolved by the Revolutionary War. Can you see any conflict between the cause that Benjamin Martin fights for in this film and the America that evolved after 1781?

Screening Notes

———————— *THE PATRIOT* ————————

VOCABULARY

dragoons   maroon

French and Indian War   militia

Gullah   regulars

Loyalists

QUESTIONS BASED ON THE FILM

1. What was the difference between the militia and the regular army?

   _____

   _____

   _____

2. How do the Rebel army commanders view the militia's performance in conventional battle formations? What alternative uses does Benjamin Martin suggest for them? How do the British view these tactics?

   _____

   _____

   _____

   _____

(continued)

3. Why is there ill will between Benjamin Martin and Major Villeneuve? Why does Benjamin not "trust the French"?

_____

_____

_____

4. Why do you think the filmmakers made Benjamin Martin a composite figure of many Revolutionary War heroes? What kinds of latitude did this give them?

_____

_____

_____

5. How does the portrayal of the British officers demonstrate the British class system of the time period? Contrast this with the American structure of forces.

_____

_____

_____

6. Why did the filmmakers choose the title *The Patriot* for this film? Would this be an appropriate title for a British audience?

_____

_____

_____

7. Keeping in mind that an important historical institution collaborated in the making of this film, comment on one scene that gave you new insight into colonial life.

_____

_____

_____

The Expansion of the New Nation

---------- TEACHER'S GUIDE ----------

AMISTAD

DreamWorks Pictures, 1997; directed by Steven Spielberg, color, 157 minutes

Note: This film is rated **R** due to violent scenes involving slavery and the Middle Passage.

BACKGROUND OF THE FILM

This film tells the story of a previously little-known event in American history: the revolt of a group of African slaves on a Spanish ship called the *Amistad,* their arrival in the United States, and the fight for their freedom that ultimately resulted in their being transported back to their homes in Africa.

Like many recent films with historical topics, *Amistad* has had more than its share of critics as well as champions. Historians have debated long and hard about what the filmakers show, what they changed, and what they left out. Some of these debates have bordered on the ridiculous, totally ignoring the fact that all history is interpretative and that this film is not meant to be a textbook.

The producers of the film state clearly that "it's a movie that blends fiction with true events" (*Amistad: A Celebration of the Film by Steven Spielberg,* New Market Press, 1998, p. 17). As a source of entertainment as well as some historical enlightenment, *Amistad* succeeds well as a vehicle for classroom viewing and discussion.

The film includes a recreation of an event that occurred in 1839. Although the international slave trade had been made illegal in Britain, Spain, and the United States by a series of treaties, the illegal importation of slaves continued. A Spanish slave hunter procured a large number of Africans in Sierra Leone and sent them on the Portuguese ship *Tecora* to Havana, Cuba.

Fifty-three Africans were bought by two Cuban planters there and shipped on the schooner *Amistad* for work on a plantation elsewhere in Cuba. The Africans mutinied during the voyage and gained control of the ship, forcing the two Cuban planters to pilot them to Africa. Instead, the planters maneuvered the ship into American waters. It was seized off the Long Island coast by a U.S. Navy ship. The two Cuban planters told authorities that the Africans were Cuban slaves (slavery itself was still legal both in Cuba and the United States) who had committed murder. Since the Africans could not be understood, their story was not told. They were jailed for murder in New Haven, Connecticut.

A Yale professor, Josiah Gibbs, was able to find a British sailor who spoke Mende (the language of the slaves), and the murder charges were dismissed. The two Cuban planters, supported by the Spanish government (whose colony Cuba was), then brought suit for the return of the Africans as their property. A complex series of court cases ensued involving rights of salvage, property rights, and international treaties. Several prominent abolitionists, including Lewis Tappan, formed the Amistad Committee to raise money to defend the Africans. The committee enlisted the help of a qualified lawyer, Roger Baldwin, who was a dedicated supporter of abolition and black education—not the bumbling real estate lawyer portrayed in the film. John Quincy Adams was also interested in the case almost from the beginning; he did not have to be coaxed to get involved.

Despite efforts by President Van Buren to extradite the Africans to Cuba to appease southern slave owners, the case of the *Amistad* Africans eventually came to the Supreme Court in January 1841. Adams and Baldwin presented their arguments. In spite of the fact that the Chief Justice of the United States, Roger Taney, was himself a slave owner, and although the Court refused to confront the moral issue of slavery, it decided in favor of the Africans. They were given their freedom.

The abolitionists, many of whom were Christian missionaries, had found homes for the Africans during the trial. They now attempted to raise money to send them home. The Africans traveled around with the abolitionists to tell their story, but the pressure of being on display caused depression among the Africans; there was even one case of suicide. Finally, in November 1841, the surviving 35 Africans, accompanied by a group of missionaries and teachers, set sail for Sierra Leone.

The film follows this basic story line but manipulates it in several ways. The abolitionists are not pictured in a flattering light; often they are portrayed as religious fanatics. Yet, it was really through their efforts that the *Amistad* captives were eventually freed. The character of Theodore Joadson is fictitious, but there were black abolitionists, such as Reverend James W.C. Pennington, who played active roles in the *Amistad* affair. Josiah Gibbs was a competent linguist; he was the one who walked the seaports looking for someone who spoke Mende. Cinqué did not participate in the creation of the defense, and he did not have the emotional meetings with Adams that are shown in the film. However, Adams met him once while the Africans were still in prison. The Africans also were not imprisoned during the entire span of the court cases, but were housed in the New Haven area. The young girls lived at the home of the jailer.

The *Amistad* Africans absorbed some Christian beliefs while in Connecticut, and students from the Yale Divinity School taught them not only religious study but also to read and write English. In fact, the Africans requested that missionaries be sent back to Sierra Leone with them. The formation of the American Missionary Association evolved from the Amistad Committee in order to support the Mendi Mission in Africa.

Many historians feel that the strength of the film is its focus on the Africans: their dignity, identity, and refusal to submit passively to their loss of freedom. The portrayal of the seizure of Cinqué by slave catchers, the horrific Middle Passage, and the revolt itself are stunning in their realistic representation of what most likely happened. The film has caused a revival of interest in the *Amistad* case, with many web sites, articles, and books dedicated to the topic, as well as the construction of a replica of the ship at Mystic Seaport in Connecticut.

The movie also brings to the fore the issue of property rights versus human rights. The Supreme Court decision was by no means an attack on the institution of slavery in the United States; rather, the Africans were set free because it was *not* proved that they were the property of the Cuban planters. If they had been judged the legal property of the Cubans, they would had been returned to them. The natural right to freedom asserted in the Declaration of Independence actually ran counter to the property rights guaranteed in the Constitution when applied to slave-ownership in the United States. This is one of the themes running through the *Amistad* affair. It has also been suggested that the character of Roger Baldwin represents "Everyman," portraying the prejudices of the time. As Baldwin learns to view the Africans less as property and more as humans, the audience participates in this revelation and is made to examine their own prejudices. (As pointed out earlier, the real Roger Baldwin was an ardent abolitionist from the beginning and not as he is shown in the film.)

Yes, historical facts are changed in *Amistad,* but they are usually done so to make the story line more interesting or to get a specific message across in a way more understandable to modern audiences. In both this film and in *Schindler's List,* director Spielberg is not afraid to tackle moral issues of timeless concern. This is what makes *Amistad* a valuable film for classroom use.

SYNOPSIS OF THE PLOT

Amistad opens with the mutiny of a group of Africans on board a ship in 1839. The crew are killed, but two Cubans are left alive to steer the ship to Africa. After six weeks, the ship is out of freshwater, and the Africans go ashore for supplies. A United States Navy ship captures the *Amistad;* the Africans are put in chains and taken to a jail in the port.

The scene switches to Spain, where the young queen, Isabella II, is told about the *Amistad* affair. The scene then switches back to the United States, where President Martin Van Buren is campaigning for reelection. In New Haven, Connecticut, black abolitionist Theodore Joadson meets with Lewis Tappan about the *Amistad* captives. They agree to arrange for legal counsel.

The Africans are brought to court before Judge Juttson. Secretary of State John Forsyth interrupts the proceedings to claim that the Africans are the "slaves" belonging to the Queen of Spain. Two naval officers then claim the Africans as their property under the laws of salvage, and the two Cuban planters also put in a claim for their "goods." A down-and-out lawyer, Roger Baldwin, convinces Tappan that since he is a property lawyer, he is the perfect man for the case. Baldwin views the Africans as stolen property, while Tappan reminds him that they are human beings who can be used by the abolitionist cause to make a statement. Tappan and Joadson also meet with John Quincy Adams to see if he will become involved in the case. He refuses.

Outside the Africans' prison, abolitionists kneel, sing, and pray—much to the bewilderment of the Africans. A linguist, Professor Gibbs, is brought in to try to communicate with the Africans, particularly with their acknowledged leader, known as Cinqué. However, the language barrier proves to be insurmountable.

Despite Baldwin's arguments that the *Amistad* captives are not from a Cuban plantation, the judge is unimpressed. Baldwin and Joadson go to the ship to search for evidence. Baldwin finds papers there that show that the *Amistad* Africans are part of the cargo of the *Tecora,* an illegal Portuguese slaver.

President Van Buren is now told that John C. Calhoun is pressuring him to execute the *Amistad* Africans and threatening the loss of support of the southern states if he doesn't. Forsyth suggests that Juttson be replaced by a younger, more insecure judge, Judge Coglin, who is more likely to bow to their wishes.

Joadson and Baldwin walk the waterfront counting in Mende to see if they can find anyone who speaks the language. They find a British ensign, James Covey, who is originally from Mendeland and can act as translator. Through Covey, Cinqué tells the story (shown in a flashback sequence) of his capture and transport to Cuba on the *Tecora*. When food runs low on the slaver, many of the captives are thrown overboard. The slave auction in Havana is also shown. Cinqué's story ends with the Africans' voyage on board the *Amistad* toward the plantation. The scene now shifts to a courtroom, where Cinqué is just finishing with his story. A British naval commander testifies to the fact that slave trading is still being conducted illegally. He corroborates Cinqué's story, despite efforts of the prosecution to discredit it. In the court, Cinqué begins to chant "Give us free!"

Judge Coglin finds in favor of the Africans and orders Ruiz and Montes, the Cuban planters, arrested for slave trading. Afraid of angering Calhoun and the southern slave owners, President Van Buren appeals the decision to the Supreme Court, which is dominated by southern justices. Cinqué is stunned by this turn of events and refuses to talk to Baldwin. Baldwin has written to John Quincy Adams, who finally appears at the prison to meet with the Africans. Adams agrees to try the case.

Cinqué meets with John Quincy Adams at his home in Massachusetts, where they discuss the case. Cinqué tells Adams that his ancestors will help him win his freedom. At the Supreme Court, Adams argues that this case is more than a property dispute; it is based upon the entire nature of man. He appeals to the "ancestors" of the American nation, including his own father, to help the justices decide. The Supreme Court decision (read by Harry A. Blackmun, an actual retired Supreme Court justice who plays the role of Justice Story) finds that the *Amistad* Africans are not property but free individuals.

The scene shifts to the liberation of the slave fortress at Lomboko and its subsequent destruction by the British navy. The last scene of the film shows the *Amistad* Africans returning to Sierra Leone. A caption tells the audience that Cinqué found his land in civil war and his family gone—possibly captured as slaves.

IDEAS FOR CLASS DISCUSSION

A good focus for class discussion would be the character of Roger Baldwin (as he is portrayed in the film), a person who changes during the time he is involved with the *Amistad* case. At first he regards the Africans as pieces of property or real estate, but later he recognizes their common humanity and is struck by their dignity and perseverance. What is the director trying to do with this characterization?

The issue of natural rights versus written property rights is a good topic for exploration. What happens when unwritten, moral law clashes with written law, as we see with the issue of liberty versus property? The horrific scenes of the Middle Passage and the slave auction certainly lend themselves to a discussion of slavery, including its economic significance, human cost, and efforts to eradicate this tragic institution.

Another focus of discussion could revolve around the ship itself. Why is it ironic that the name of the ship, *La Amistad,* means "friendship"?

BOOKS AND MATERIALS RELATING TO THIS FILM AND TOPIC

Amistad: *"Give Us Free": A Celebration of The Film by Steven Spielberg.* New York: Newmarket Press, 1998.

Davis, Natalie Zemon. *Slaves on Screen: Film and Historical Vision.* Cambridge, MA: Harvard University Press, 2000.

The History Teacher, 31, no. 3, May, 1998. This edition contains a special section about the film and its use by teachers.

Jones, Howard. *Mutiny on the* Amistad: *The Saga of a Slave Revolt and its Impact on American Abolition, Law and Diplomacy.* Rev. ed. New York: Oxford University Press, 1997.

There are many excellent web sites about the *Amistad* case, including one at the National Archives that includes teaching materials. Consult your search engine for current URLs using the key word *Amistad.*

OTHER MEDIA RESOURCES FOR THIS TIME PERIOD

Many of the films covering the early nineteenth century in the United States are problematic in that filmmakers seem to be infatuated with the romance and legend of this time period and often sacrifice historical accuracy in order to tell a good story. Thus, figures like Daniel Boone, Dolly Madison, Davy Crockett, and Andrew Jackson have evolved into folk heroes; it becomes difficult to separate myth from fact.

The Alamo (1960, 199 minutes) John Wayne's epic, if somewhat tendentious, recreation of the holding action that gave Texas time to organize its defense against Mexico

The Buccaneer (1958, 121 minutes) Romanticized story of pirate Jean Lafitte and the help he gave Andrew Jackson at the Battle of New Orleans during the War of 1812

Davy Crockett: King of the Wild Frontier (1955, 93 minutes) Exemplifies the larger-than-life hero popular in this period of American history

Gangs of New York (2002, 160 minutes) Martin Scorcese film about street gangs in New York City between 1846 and 1863; rated **R**

Gone to Texas (1986, 144 minutes) Made-for-TV movie focusing on Sam Houston and the heroes of Texas independence

One Man's Hero (1988, 122 minutes) Story of the Saint Patrick Battalion of Irish immigrants who deserted to Mexico during the Mexican War; rated **R**

Race to Freedom: The Story of the Underground Railroad (1994, 90 minutes) Story of slaves in pre-Civil War America who risk everything for a chance to gain their freedom through the secret network known as the Underground Railroad

--- **AMISTAD** ---

DreamWorks Pictures, 1997; directed by Steven Spielberg

Major Character	Actor/Actress
Cinqué (Sengbe Pieh)	Djimon Hounsou
Roger S. Baldwin	Matthew McConaughey
Theodore Joadson	Morgan Freeman
Lewis Tappan	Stellan Skarsgard
John Quincy Adams	Anthony Hopkins
Martin Van Buren	Nigel Hawthorne
Ensign Covey	Chjwetel Ejiofor

WHAT TO WATCH FOR

Amistad is a film that tells a little-known story in American history—the mutiny of a group of Africans onboard a ship transporting them to a life of slavery, their imprisonment in New Haven, Connecticut, and the court case that ultimately granted them their freedom and allowed them to return to their homeland. Since the film's debut, interest in the *Amistad* affair has grown. Much research has been done about the events surrounding the case.

It is important to understand that the *Amistad* case was not decided on the basis of the evils of slavery, but rather as a case involving property rights. Slavery was legal in Spanish territories as well as in the United States in 1839, although the slave trade from Africa had been outlawed by Congress in 1807 and by international treaty in 1817. In the *Antelope* case in 1825, the U.S. Supreme Court recognized the right of foreigners to trade in slaves if their own countries permitted it. The *Amistad* case revolved around whether the jailed Africans were the legal property of Cuban slave owners or whether they were Africans who had been illegally captured, enslaved, and sent to Cuba in violation of international law.

(continued)

The film contains several distortions of history. It makes the court case, especially the presentation by John Quincy Adams, look like more of a crusade against slavery than it actually was. It also portrays the abolitionists as religious fanatics who were more interested in their cause than in the well-being of the *Amistad* Africans as individuals. In reality, it was the abolitionists, led by Lewis Tappan, who formed the Amistad Committee and raised money for the defense of the Africans. The abolitionists also tended to their housing and other needs, and they eventually funded the Africans' return to Africa. Roger Baldwin was not the money-grubbing, down-and-out lawyer portrayed in the film; he was a dedicated abolitionist and successful attorney. Theodore Joadson (played by Morgan Freeman) is a fictitious character, although there were African-American abolitionists who worked diligently for the cause. Despite the leadership really shown by Cinqué among the Africans, he did not participate with Adams in working on the defense presented to the Supreme Court.

Where the film is strongest is in its depiction of the capture of Cinqué, the horrific Middle Passage, and the slave auction in Cuba. The director also went to great lengths to hire African actors from the same geographic area that was the homeland of the *Amistad* captives. An authority on Mende language and culture was brought in to make certain that the *Amistad* Africans in the film spoke the correct dialect.

To give the film a certain aesthetic look, Steven Spielberg decided to study the colors of the paintings of Francisco Goya, an early nineteenth-century Spanish artist whose work shows a dark and somber quality. It was also decided not to use complicated camera moves; there are no fancy tracking or crane shots. The director wanted the movie to have a still, "tableau" quality to it. Mystic Seaport in Connecticut was used for harbor shots, and Newport, Rhode Island, was transformed into nineteenth-century New Haven. El Morro, a sixteenth-century fortress in Puerto Rico, was used for the scenes of Lomboko, the slave fortress where Cinqué is brought as a captive. The prison where the *Amistad* Africans are kept was constructed on a Los Angeles sound stage.

This movie was passed over by the Academy Awards® Committee and received no recognition. *Titanic* was the big winner that year. It has been suggested that the subject matter of *Amistad* made it too serious for most audiences and less of a box-office draw.

─── **AMISTAD** ───

VOCABULARY

abolitionist   Middle Passage

barracoon

QUESTIONS BASED ON THE FILM

1. It has been suggested that the character of Roger Baldwin is portrayed as "Everyman," representing the audience's prejudices and misconceptions. How does Baldwin change during the course of the film?

_____

_____

_____

2. If the slave trade was declared illegal in Britain, the United States, and the Spanish colonies before 1839, why did Spain want the *Amistad* Africans returned?

_____

_____

3. In order for the *Amistad* Africans to receive their freedom, what has to be proved? In other words, what is the focus of the court case surrounding them?

_____

_____

(continued)

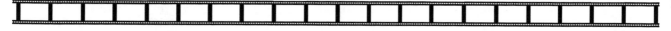

4. What are President Martin Van Buren's concerns about the *Amistad* case? Whom is he trying to appease?

_____

_____

_____

5. How is the problem of communication with the Africans resolved? How is this crucial to their cause?

_____

_____

_____

6. In his speech to the Supreme Court, John Quincy Adams states in the film, "Give us the courage to do what is right—and if it means civil war? Then let it come. And when it does, may it be, finally, the last battle of the American Revolution."

   What issue does Adams see as unresolved in the United States at that time? What does he mean by this speech?

_____

_____

_____

7. Why is it ironic that it is a British ship that destroys the slave fortress at Lomboko?

_____

_____

_____

_____

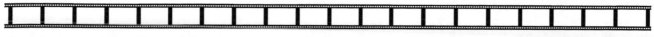

TEACHER'S GUIDE

GLORY

Tri-Star Pictures, 1989; directed by Edward Zwick, color, 122 minutes; received Academy Awards for Best Supporting Actor (Denzel Washington), Best Cinematography, and Best Sound.

Note: Although this film is rated **R** due to violence, it is featured in school catalogs. You may wish to use a parental permission form.

BACKGROUND OF THE FILM

Glory has been hailed as one of the most historically accurate and realistic movies about the American Civil War. It is also a film that presents an aspect of history that is unknown to most Americans—the fact that by the end of the Civil War, African-American soldiers made up twelve percent of the Union Army. There were 166 African-American regiments in the Union Army and over 180,000 African-American soldiers, many of whom had been slaves until within a few months of their enlistment.

Glory focuses on the formation of the Massachusetts 54th Regiment, its training, its efforts to be used in combat rather than as a labor force, and finally the 54th's heroic attack on Fort Wagner, South Carolina. The assault on Fort Wagner by the 600 men of the 54th was a turning point for the United States' recruitment of African-American soldiers and, in many respects, a turning point in the fight for the abolition of slavery. As one abolitionist commented: "Who asks now in doubt and derision, 'Will the Negro fight?' The answer is spoken from the cannon's mouth . . . it comes to us from . . . those graves beneath Fort Wagner's walls, which the American people will surely never forget." (James M. McPherson, "The 'Glory' Story: The 54th Massachusetts and the Civil War," *The New Republic* 202, nos. 2–3 (January 8 and 15, 1990: 23).

Robert Gould Shaw was the son of prominent Boston abolitionists. He quit Harvard in his junior year to join the Union Army. He was wounded at Antietam Creek in 1862 and became disillusioned by the savagery of the bloodshed. When Massachusetts Governor John Albion Andrew, encouraged by the black leader Frederick Douglass, commissioned an all-African American regiment, 23-year-old Shaw was offered the command. Douglass's two sons enlisted in the 54th, and Lewis Douglass was sergeant-major of the regiment from its beginning, a fact not brought out by the film.

Shaw is the only principal character in the film who is not fictitious. Some historians have wondered why real historical characters were not used, such as Garth Wilkinson James, brother of William and Henry James, who was the adjutant of the regiment; the Douglass brothers; or Sergeant William H. Carney, the first African American to win the Congressional Medal of Honor for heroism. Moreover, where the movie gives the impression that most of the soldiers of the 54th were former slaves, the regiment was predominantly made up of African Americans from the North who had always been free. It is true that most of the 180,000 African-American soldiers who eventually served in the Union Army were former slaves, and *Glory* can be understood as an attempt to universalize the 54th's experience.

Despite a few inaccuracies, such as the 54th attacking the fort from the north instead of from the south, attention was paid to the historical detail of the events themselves. Civil War historian/novelist Shelby Foote acted as a consultant on the film. The African-American soldiers, with Shaw's support, did refuse to accept unequal pay. (Congress approved equal pay in 1864.) The shoes actually delivered to the men had no left or right; they simply wore them until they became left and right. The close order of the battle lines shown with the massing of men shoulder to shoulder is what accounted for the high casualties during the Civil War. Civil War reenactors were used, including 38 African-American reenactors. Reenactors are Civil War buffs who have authentic uniforms and weapons and participate in recreations or reenactments of Civil War battles. Colonel Shaw did dismount his horse and lead his men in attacking the fort. His body was thrown into a common grave with his men. When a Union commander requested the return of Shaw's body, a Confederate officer replied, "We have buried him with his niggers." Later, when a Union officer tried to recover the body, Shaw's father wrote to stop him, saying that this was the most appropriate burial place for his son, the field where he had fallen.

There is a monument in Boston to Shaw and the 54th Regiment sculpted in bas-relief by Augustus St. Gaudens, showing the colonel on his horse surrounded by his proudly marching men. The closing credits of the movie are run-over shots of this monument.

In addition to the fictionalized (and, some charge, stereotypical) characters and the overemphasis on escaped slaves within the ranks of the 54th, critics of the film have questioned the centering of the story on Shaw and his white subordinates, rather than on the African Americans who, in order to fight for freedom, struggled against Northern prejudice and Southern threats that they would not be treated as war prisoners if captured bearing arms against the Confederacy. Finally, since the film ends in the bloody and unsuccessful Fort Wagner battle, the film inevitably raises the question of the meaning of the term "glory" itself, juxtaposing all the heroic paraphernalia of traditional war films' climaxes against the futility and slaughter of the event itself. Interestingly, movie critics mostly questioned the casting of the obviously youthful and uncommanding Matthew Broderick as Colonel Shaw, because it ran counter to the conventions of heroic commanders in the expectations of Hollywood.

SYNOPSIS OF THE PLOT

The movie opens at Antietam Creek, Maryland, in 1862. Twenty-three-year-old Robert Gould Shaw is wounded during the Confederate rout of Union forces. In a field hospital, Shaw hears that Lincoln is going to free the slaves.

At home in Boston, Shaw meets Frederick Douglass and Governor Andrew at a reception. The governor proposes to raise a regiment of Negro soldiers; Shaw's name has been submitted as commander. Shaw's friend, Cabot Forbes, chides him for accepting, but ends up joining him.

Shaw surveys his prospective troops, who include his well-educated friend Thomas Searles as well as illiterate field hands. They are marched to a camp at Readville, Massachusetts, just outside Boston, past white soldiers making derisive comments. To train and bring discipline to the unit, Shaw brings in a tough Irish drill sergeant named Mulcahy.

The government finally sends guns to the regiment, and Shaw drills them in the proper use of the weapons. Forbes confronts Shaw about why he is treating the men so harshly.

Shaw goes to the officers' mess for Christmas, where his fellow officers are condescending to him because of his command of the 54th. Meanwhile, Trip, one of Shaw's men, has deserted to find some shoes. He is captured and Shaw orders him publicly flogged. Another of Shaw's men, Rawlins, informs Shaw that shoes are a necessity; Shaw goes to the quartermaster to get shoes, by force if necessary, for his men. He is successful.

When payday arrives, Shaw reads a letter from the government that the regiment will be paid $10 per month, $3 less than white soldiers. The soldiers refuse to accept any pay, and Shaw rips up his pay as well. The long-awaited uniforms arrive, and the 54th marches down the main street of Boston to its first assignment.

The 54th is sent south, and Rawlins is made a sergeant major. The men arrive in Beaufort, South Carolina, on June 9, 1863. There is very little action there and it becomes clear that they are only to be used as a labor force. Shaw finally confronts the commanding officer at Beaufort with the knowledge of irregularities and forces him to transfer his men to a combat unit. At James Island, they meet and repel a Confederate force.

The Union commanders decide to try to take Fort Wagner, a coastal installation that protects Charleston, South Carolina. Shaw volunteers the 54th to lead the attack, an almost suicidal task due to the lack of cover along the open sandy beach that must be crossed and the ocean limiting maneuvering room. The men sing spirituals that night and prepare themselves for battle.

As Shaw's men march by the white soldiers, they are cheered. Shaw sends his horse back to the Union lines and joins his men on foot. They charge Fort Wagner, get to the dunes, then wait until dark when they mount the attack on the fort's sand parapets under fierce bombardment. Shaw is killed going up the embankment, but his troops fight on. The next day, the dead of the 54th cover the beach. They have failed to take the fort. The Confederates bury Shaw with his men in a mass grave. Closing graphics state that the fort was never taken, but that the conduct of the 54th Regiment was an important breakthrough in the acceptance of black troops in the war.

IDEAS FOR CLASS DISCUSSION

The film's title itself can serve as a discussion topic, especially in light of the reemergence of the virtues of military prowess in the wake of the "techno-war" in the Persian Gulf and Afghanistan. Why was the film titled *Glory*? In what sense is what happened to these men glorious? Is the term used positively or cynically? Other topics might include the questions raised by critics about the liberties taken by the filmmakers with the recreation of the battle for Fort Wagner itself, the focus of the film on the regiment's Caucasian officers, and the substitution of stereotypical characters for portrayals of the real African Americans who went to war for the Union in the Civil War.

BOOKS AND MATERIALS RELATING TO THIS FILM AND TOPIC

Benson, Richard. *Lay This Laurel.* Commentary by Lincoln Kirstein. New York: Eakins Press Foundation, 1973.

Burchard, Peter. *Glory.* New York: St. Martin's Press, 1989.

Burchard, Peter. *One Gallant Rush.* New York: St. Martin's Press, 1989.

McPherson, James M. *Battle Cry of Freedom: The Civil War Era.* New York: Oxford University Press, 1988.

McPherson, James M. "The 'Glory' Story: The 54th Massachusetts and the Civil War." *The New Republic* 202, nos. 2–3 (January 8 and 15, 1990): 22–28.

Pyron, Darolen Asbury, ed. *Recasting: "Gone with the Wind" in American Culture.* Miami: University Presses of Florida, 1983.

OTHER MEDIA RESOURCES FOR THIS TIME PERIOD

Abe Lincoln of Illinois (1940, 110 minutes) The film version of Robert E. Sherwood's reverential play with Raymond Massey reprising his Broadway triumph as the young Illinois lawyer matured by the loss of his great love; it is mostly faithful to the history on which it is based.

Across Five Aprils (1986, 29 minutes) Dramatizes the effects of the Civil War on the home front; based on the story by Irene Hunt

The Andersonville Trial (1970, 150 minutes) An excellent PBS Hollywood Television Theater version of the 1865 war-crimes trial of a Confederate captain held responsible for the deaths from starvation or disease of some 15,000 Union prisoners of war; it was based on MacKinley Kantor's novel.

Denmark Vesey's Rebellion (1981, 90 minutes) About an abortive slave revolt in South Carolina in 1822; *Solomon Northrup's Odyssey* (1984, 120 minutes) about a free African American kidnapped into slavery in Louisiana until rescued in 1853; and *Experiment in Freedom: Charlotte Foster's Mission* (1985, 125 minutes) about a wealthy Philadelphia woman who risks everything to start a community of freed slaves on the South Carolina sea islands during the Civil War are three parts of the PBS *A House Divided* series on which historian Robert Toplin worked.

The General (1927, 74 minutes) Buster Keaton's silent classic about the unsuccessful 1862 attempt by Union spies, led by James J. Andrews, to steal a Confederate train near Atlanta and run it to Chattanooga, destroying bridges, supply depots, and telegraph lines as they went; they were pursued and most were captured and hanged (a fate omitted from the film) by Confederates in other trains. A more serious sound version of the story, called *The Great Locomotive Chase* (1956, 85 minutes) also exists.

Gettysburg (1993, 261 minutes) Turner Pictures epic based upon Michael Shaara's novel *Killer Angels* about the most decisive battle of the Civil War

Gone with the Wind (1939, 219 minutes) David O. Selznick's film of Margaret Mitchell's novel spectacularly recreates Sherman's destruction of Atlanta. But, in order to walk a fine line between depression and preparedness values, and between northern liberal and southern conservative opinion, Selznick presented a sanitized, nostalgic, and, in some ways, simple-minded antebellum South in contrast to the complex ambivalence about the South, its family traditions, and its "peculiar institution" of the Mitchell novel. The film's script and production values reflect a moment in the history of American and Hollywood consciousness and of the Southern renaissance of the 1930s as much (or more) than they do the history of the Civil War. Precisely because this film (especially since its recent restored theatrical rerelease) is so much a part of many people's unconscious vision of the Civil War, if it is shown, it should be screened with great care.

The Horse Soldiers (1959, 119 minutes) John Ford's recasting of Union Colonel Benjamin H. Grierson's 1,700-man raid 300 miles inside Mississippi to cut Confederate supply lines to Vicksburg; unlike John Wayne's rough-hewn portrayal of Colonel Marlow, a railroad engineer, Grierson was actually an Illinois music teacher before the war. But scenes like the Union destruction of Newton Station and the attack by Confederate military-school students on the Union force are reflections of fact, though, unlike the film, the Northern forces actually cut them down.

The Red Badge of Courage (1951, 70 minutes) Directed by John Huston and starring Audie Murphy, this version of Stephen Crane's novel portrays the experiences of a young soldier in the Civil War.

The True Story of Glory Continues (1991, 45 minutes) The background and continuation video produced as a companion piece to the film *Glory*

GLORY

Tri-Star Pictures, 1989; directed by Edward Zwick

Major Character	Actor/Actress
Colonel Robert Gould Shaw	Matthew Broderick
John Rawlins	Morgan Freeman
Trip	Denzel Washington
Cabot Forbes	Cary Elwes
Thomas Searles	André Braugher
Shirts	Jihmi Kennedy
Sergeant Mulcahy	John Finn

WHAT TO WATCH FOR

Glory tells the little-known story of the formation of one of the first all-African-American regiments during the Civil War and its heroic assault on Fort Wagner, South Carolina. The 54th Massachusetts Regiment was formed in Boston at the urging of abolitionists and the prominent African-American leader Frederick Douglass, who is briefly portrayed in the film. Douglass felt it was important that African Americans take part in a war that, especially after the Emancipation Proclamation, was being fought to gain their freedom. It was also hoped that African-American regiments would dispel the stereotype of African Americans as lazy, shiftless, and cowardly. Watch for examples of this stereotyping in the film. The gallant assault on Fort Wagner proved the courage and discipline of the African-American regiments, and by the end of the war, African-American soldiers made up twelve percent of the total Union forces.

Despite the impression given by the movie, most of the 54th Regiment were Northern African Americans who had been free all their lives. Some Northern African Americans were well educated, like the character Thomas Searles. It is true,

(continued)

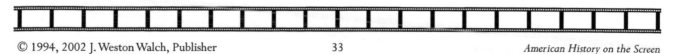

however, that most of the soldiers in the 166 African-American regiments who fought in the Civil War had been slaves up until a few months before their enlistment.

This film does present an accurate picture of the Civil War era, particularly the method of fighting. Note how close the battle lines are with a massing of the soldiers shoulder to shoulder. This is what accounts for the terrible casualty rate of the Civil War, one of the highest in history. The willing sacrifice of the 54th at Fort Wagner created new levels of respect for the abilities and courage of African-American soldiers throughout the Union Army. The 54th's "glory" also raises disturbing questions about the nature of war itself, about the Fort Wagner tactics, and about the pointlessness of such sacrifices as a means of gaining respect. Fort Wagner remained in Confederate hands until the end of the war, and after the brief Reconstruction period, African-American soldiers were reduced to menial tasks and garrison duty except on the American frontier, where they performed heroically in the Indian wars.

Glory has stimulated interest in the role played by the black regiments in the Civil War, a previously forgotten chapter in African-American history. "Reenactors," Civil War buffs who recreate the battles and camp life of the 1860s, now include more African-American members among their ranks than before the release of this film.

Screening Notes

UNIT 4

The Civil War

GLORY

VOCABULARY

abolitionist

bayonet

Confederate

contraband

Emancipation Proclamation

Union

QUESTIONS BASED ON THE FILM

1. Describe how the method of fighting during the Civil War contributed to the high casualty rate.

   _____

   _____

   _____

2. According to Shaw, how are the black troops different from the white troops in their use of leisure time and in their attitude?

   _____

   _____

   _____

3. What is the purpose of the proclamation that Shaw reads from the Confederate Congress?

   _____

   _____

(continued)

4. Why is flogging so particularly humiliating to Trip?

_____

_____

_____

5. How does the white officer of the contraband troops think secession can be cured?

_____

_____

_____

6. How does the attitude of the white combat troops change towards the 54th?

_____

_____

_____

7. Why do you think the filmmakers chose to call their movie "Glory"?

_____

_____

_____

_____

TEACHER'S GUIDE

DANCES WITH WOLVES

Orion Pictures, 1990; directed by Kevin Costner, color, 180 minutes; nominated for 12 Academy Awards®, film won Best Picture, Best Director, Best Cinematography, and four other Oscars

BACKGROUND OF THE FILM

This award-winning film was actor Kevin Costner's first effort as a director. It is a monumental work costing $18 million, which Costner raised partly from overseas investors. The film was a gamble for Orion Pictures, a financially weak studio, and many referred to the movie while it was in production as "Costner's Last Stand."

The logistics of shooting this movie presented an awesome task for the novice director, who had to find and take charge of 3,500 American bison, 300 horses, 2 wolves, 42 wagons, 36 tepees, 500 extras, and 130 crew members. Shooting took 5 months, from July to November, at 27 different locations in South Dakota, where temperatures were often over 100 degrees in summer and 20 degrees in late fall. Six months were spent in preproduction and research. To assure historical accuracy, Costner hired an American Indian artifact historian, Cathy Smith. Smith was kept on hand for every shot to make certain that the costumes and rituals were correct. The costumes were made using traditional Sioux skills, such as brain tanning (using liquefied animal brains to soften skins) to provide authenticity. Even the war paint was based on traditional designs. American Indian artifact restorer Larry Belitz was in charge of creating an 1860s Lakota village

with the correct tepees, cooking utensils, and weapons. Even the arrows were made of the same wood—red willow or chokecherry—used by the Sioux. Much of the movie's dialogue is in the Sioux dialect Lakota, with English subtitles. Because none of the American Indians knew Lakota, they, along with Kevin Costner and Mary McDonnell, were tutored by Doris Leader Charge, an instructor in Lakota studies. One result of the movie has been an increased interest by younger Sioux in learning their tribal language.

This film has been hailed as a major attempt to redress the many erroneous portrayals of American Indians through the years in films and television. Often portrayed either as bloodthirsty savages or half-wits speaking in grunts, American Indians have been exploited and stereotyped in most of the old-time Hollywood Westerns. Costner wanted only Native Americans to portray the Sioux in his film, and although not all of the actors used were Lakota, they were all American Indians. The Sioux are portrayed as real people, making mistakes, laughing, worrying, and making love.

Dances with Wolves has also been hailed as the first environmental Western—one that concerns itself with our treatment of nature. The role of animals is particularly noteworthy; they become integral characters in the story. Note particularly that while the Lakota hunt buffalo only to secure their survival needs, they are killed by the encroaching whites not for food, but for their tongues and hides. The wolf who befriends Dunbar is killed by the soldiers for no reason other than sport. In its examination of the past, the film speaks to the present fouling of the planet as well.

This film was not without its detractors. Some critics felt that the film was wrong in portraying all whites, with the exception of Dunbar, as evil, demented, and/or rapacious, and the American Indians as the embodiment of virtue. Other critics felt that the film was too politically correct in its portrayal of the nineteenth-century frontier; that Dunbar spoke like a twentieth-century political activist transported back to the 1860s and was thus unrealistic for the time the film portrayed.

These criticisms, as well as the many other issues the film itself raises, make this film an excellent springboard for discussion. Treatment of native peoples and their portrayal in media certainly could be one topic. Another topic could be the role of the frontier in American thought and the idea of progress through conquest and expansion, or through unlimited resource exploitation. Frederick Jackson Turner could certainly be used as a source here. *Dances with Wolves* inverts the frontier myth by portraying it as a process of loss and wanton destruction; it portrays the frontier itself not as an empty place awaiting settlement, but as a place inhabited by a people in harmony with their environment, ferociously displaced by ignorant and greedy interlopers who win because of their more powerful weapons of destruction. The myth of manifest destiny is a pervasive one in our history and could be examined through the film.

SYNOPSIS OF THE PLOT

The film opens at a Civil War battlefield in Tennessee in 1863. Union soldier John Dunbar has been wounded. Rather than wait to have his leg amputated, he steals a horse and rides unarmed along the no-man's-land between the Union and Confederate lines, tempting fate by challenging the Confederates to fire. He survives and is decorated for heroism. Upon recovering from his wound, he is allowed to pick a new post. Dunbar assigns himself to the furthermost edge of the frontier, because he wants to experience it "before it disappears." But the demented officer who assigns him to Fort Sedgewick and arranges for

his transport commits suicide immediately thereafter, and when Dunbar's guide is killed by American Indians after dropping him and the outpost's supplies at Fort Sedgewick, there is no one left who knows of Dunbar's posting. When he arrives, he finds the fort is deserted, but he is determined to stay on with only the company of his horse Cisco and a wolf he names Two Socks. American Indians spy him playing with the latter. Dunbar rebuilds the fort and cleans up a garbage dump he finds nearby.

American Indians visit the fort and attempt to steal Cisco but are unsuccessful. Dunbar decides to meet with the American Indians and establish contact. He comes across a young American Indian woman who is hurt. He discovers that she is white. When he brings her to the camp, the American Indians tell him to go away—he is not welcome. The American Indians decide they should deal with this lone white man. Chief Ten Bears sends Kicking Bird and Wind in His Hair to the fort. The meetings go well. The white woman in the Lakota tribe, whose name is Stands with a Fist, is coaxed into acting as interpreter for Dunbar, although she has not spoken English since she was five years old.

One night, Dunbar wakes to a thundering sound. It is a herd of buffalo. Dunbar rides to the camp to tell the American Indians, who immediately move out in search of the herd. The tribe comes across many rotting buffalo carcasses; white hunters have slaughtered them for their skins. When the herd is spotted, the Lakota hunt the buffalo for their meat. Dunbar is included in the hunt and the subsequent feasting to celebrate its success. He begins to spend more and more time with the Sioux.

When a Pawnee war party attacks the Sioux camp, Dunbar gets guns and ammunition from the fort to help his friends defend themselves. Dunbar is given an American Indian name, "Dances with Wolves," and marries Stands with a Fist in a Sioux wedding ceremony.

The tribe packs and begins to move to winter camp, but Dunbar, in a makeshift costume, half Indian, half soldier, makes one last trip to Fort

Sedgewick to retrieve his journal. When he arrives at the fort, he finds it occupied by soldiers. The soldiers shoot Cisco and capture Dunbar, who they presume is a traitor. An illiterate soldier who has found his journal uses its pages as toilet paper. They send Dunbar to Fort Hays to be tried and hanged, but he is rescued by the Sioux and reunited with the tribe. He fears that the soldiers will hunt for him and avenge themselves on the tribe and urges the Sioux to move their camp. He and Stands with a Fist leave the tribe to eliminate the threat. When the soldiers do arrive, the Sioux camp is deserted.

Note: There is a longer version of this movie available on DVD. The book *Dances with Wolves, The Illustrated Story of the Epic Film* has a plot synopsis that contains scenes cut during the editing of the film that may be added to the video version.

IDEAS FOR CLASS DISCUSSION

This unit is an excellent springboard for a discussion about how Native Americans have been portrayed in films and on television. Many films in the past had American Indians speaking almost babytalk or in unintelligible grunts. Why do you think this film uses subtitles? How does this affect the viewer and his or her perception of the Lakota people? Related to this might be a discussion of how the Lakota people themselves are portrayed. It is certainly a far cry from the usual portrayal of Native Americans in films—as uncivilized savages. The class might discuss whether this portrayal has swung the pendulum too far in the opposite direction. Another discussion topic is one about the character of John Dunbar and whether he is a 1990s persona in a nineteenth-century setting. Is it likely that a person at that time would be so environmentally aware and sensitive to the virtues of the peoples he encountered?

BOOKS AND MATERIALS RELATING TO THIS FILM AND TOPIC

Brown, Dee A. *Bury My Heart at Wounded Knee: An Indian History of the American West.* New York: Henry Holt and Co., 1971.

Connell, Evan S. *Son of the Morning Star: Custer and the Little Bighorn.* San Francisco: North Point Press, 1984. A 1991 two-part, made-for-television movie was based upon this book.

Costner, Kevin, Michael Blake, and Jim Wilson. *Dances with Wolves: The Illustrated Story of the Epic Film.* New York: Newmarket Press, 1990.

Friar, Ralph L., and Natasha Friar. *The Only Good Indian . . . The Hollywood Gospel.* New York: Drama Book Specialists, 1972.

OTHER MEDIA RESOURCES FOR THIS TIME PERIOD

Buffalo Soldiers (1997, 95 minutes) A made-for-TV movie starring Danny Glover about the racial tensions between black and white soldiers in the American West after the Civil War

Cheyenne Autumn (1964, 156 minutes) This film has been compared to *Dances with Wolves* in that it shows the American government's policy of genocide towards American Indians.

In Pursuit of Honor (1995, 110 minutes) A made-for-TV movie about a group of cavalry officers who disobey the orders of General Douglas McArthur to destroy hundreds of army horses

The Last of His Tribe (1992, 113 minutes) A made-for-TV movie about Ishi, the last surviving Indian of his California tribe

Little Big Man (1970, 150 minutes) The sole survivor of Custer's Last Stand relates his life story in both the American Indian and white man's worlds

You Know My Name (1998, 94 minutes) True story about early film director/producer Bill Tilghman who was a real life cowboy before coming to Hollywood

UNIT 5

The West

───── *DANCES WITH WOLVES* ─────

Orion Pictures, 1990; directed by Kevin Costner

Major Character	Actor/Actress
Lieutenant John J. Dunbar	Kevin Costner
Kicking Bird	Graham Greene
Stands with a Fist	Mary McDonnell
Wind in His Hair	Rodney A. Grant
Ten Bears	Floyd Red Crow Westerman
Black Shawl	Tantoo Cardinal
Smiles a Lot	Nathan Lee Chasing His Horse
Stone Calf	Jimmy Herman

WHAT TO WATCH FOR

Dances with Wolves was produced and directed by Kevin Costner, who also played the part of the main character, John Dunbar. This epic film won seven Academy Awards® including Best Picture.

This film has been hailed by many historians as one that redresses many wrongs in Hollywood's portrayal of American Indians. Costner went to great lengths to provide an accurate picture of Sioux (or, as these people called themselves, Lakota) life. Specialists versed in Sioux culture were hired to make certain that costumes, rituals, and props were authentic. The language spoken by the Sioux in the film with English subtitles is Lakota. A professor of Lakota studies from Sinte Gloska College in South Dakota taught crew members, including the native Sioux, Lakota for the film. One result of the popularity of this film has been a renewed interest in the Lakota language and culture by many Sioux.

(continued)

The film has also been hailed as the first environmental Western. Dunbar searches for the unspoiled frontier; he wishes to see it before it is gone. Compare the ways in which the American Indians inhabit the land with the ways in which white settlers, soldiers, and hunters occupy it.

Animals play a very important role in the movie. One reason that Costner selected South Dakota as the location for shooting was the proximity of the world's largest privately owned herd of buffalo. Two trained buffalo (Mammoth, owned by rock singer Neil Young, and Cody, the mascot of a meat company) were also used. The scene where a buffalo charges a fallen boy is actually Cody racing toward an Oreo cookie, his favorite treat, held out of camera range by a trainer. The fallen buffalo are wire-framed fur dummies. No animals were harmed to make this film.

This movie has also generated some controversy. Some critics accused Costner of making the American Indians too virtuous and the whites too evil. Others felt that Dunbar's sensibilities were those of a twentieth-century person and that the film transferred 1990s values into the world of the 1860s, when the environment was seen simply as a resource to be tamed and exploited for human benefit.

Screening Notes

--- *DANCES WITH WOLVES* ---

VOCABULARY

frontier   medicine man

garrison   Tatonka (buffalo)

Pawnee   tipi

Sioux

QUESTIONS BASED ON THE FILM

1. Why does Dunbar end up at Fort Sedgewick?

_____

_____

_____

2. What is the significance of Dunbar's discovery of the garbage dump near the fort?

_____

_____

_____

3. Why is Stands with a Fist afraid of Dunbar at first?

_____

_____

_____

(continued)

4. Why has this film been labeled the first environmental Western?

_____

_____

_____

5. How does Dunbar compare the warfare among American Indian tribes to the Civil War in which he has participated?

_____

_____

_____

6. What kind of helmet does Ten Bears show Dunbar? What are Ten Bears' fears?

_____

_____

_____

7. What devices or techniques does the film use to draw you sympathetically into Lakota life and culture? How do they help you understand the American Indian view of the relationship between human beings and their environment?

_____

_____

_____

8. Why is Dunbar accused of treason?

_____

_____

_____

UNIT 6

The Immigrant
Experience and the
Turn of the Century

TEACHER'S GUIDE

HESTER STREET

Midwest Films, 1975; directed by Joan Micklin Silver, black and white, 90 minutes

BACKGROUND OF THE FILM

At the end of the nineteenth and during the early years of the twentieth century, immigration to the United States, which was being encouraged, was at its peak. This was an outgrowth of American expansion and industrialization. Although the United States has always been a nation built upon immigration, the sheer volume of people who entered the country at that time made this era unique. *Hester Street* is a simply made yet effective film about the immigrant experience. It particularly explores the problems of assimilation in a new land, using as its focus a young family of Russian Jews.

In nineteenth-century Eastern Europe, Jews were traditionally forced to live in an area known as the Pale of Settlement, a region covering eastern Germany, Austria, Romania, and western Russia. After the assassination of Russian Czar Alexander II in 1881, forced "Russification" programs were instituted, and Jews were increasingly scapegoated as the source of Russia's troubles. There were pogroms (organized campaigns of violence against Jews) in 1881–82, 1891, and 1905–06. Because of these oppressions, Jewish emigration from Russia and Eastern Europe rose dramatically. Annual Jewish immigration to the United States peaked at about 258,000 in 1907.

Jews were among the earliest immigrants to the Americas. A number of German Jews who immigrated in the first half of the nineteenth century became successfully assimilated into the East Coast middle class and participated in the American economic and geographic expansion. The Eastern European Jewish immigrants who arrived later settled in New York City; most came through recently opened Ellis Island. They were distinctive in their dress and habits, and they lived in crowded ethnic neighborhoods in five- or six-story walk-up tenements, often without hot water and usually with just one toilet per floor. In 1910, about 500,000 Jews were crowded into the 1.5 square miles of the Lower East Side of New York.

When they came to this country, Eastern European Jews tended to cluster in neighborhoods where they spoke Yiddish. They communicated only with other Jews and worked primarily for other Jews, mostly in the "needle trades." For example, probably three fourths of the garment workers in New York City before World War I were Eastern European Jews.

All of this is reflected in the film: the crowded conditions of the Lower East Side, the garment trade where Jake makes his living, and the ethnicity of the neighborhood. The director adapted the screenplay from a story by Abraham Cahan titled "Yekl." Cahan was a Jewish immigrant who arrived in New York in 1882. A Socialist, he was forced to leave Russia to avoid the persecution of dissidents following the assassination of the czar. Cahan was the founding editor of a Yiddish-language newspaper called the *Jewish Daily Forward,* which is still published today.

Joan Micklin Silver had such a difficult time finding support for her film that her husband ended up acting as the distributor. She had the good fortune to find superb actors; Carol Kane, who plays the character of Gitl, was nominated for an Academy Award® for Best Actress. The fact that the film is shot in black and white adds to the period feel of the piece, despite the fact that the boom microphone is often seen at the top of the frame. The background music is ragtime, which was becoming popular at the time. Much of the dialogue is in Yiddish with English subtitles, which adds to the authenticity of the film. (The Yiddish language evolved between the ninth and twelfth centuries; it was originally a German dialect written in Hebrew. As time went on, Hebrew words were added as well as terms from other European languages, and Yiddish became a unifying language for Eastern European Jews.)

The main themes of the film involve the value and different rates of assimilation and the resulting acculturation gap that can develop among family members. Often there was a gender difference in the rate of assimilation. Men, being out in the work force and more in contact with people beyond their immediate group, tended to Americanize more quickly than their wives, who tended to do piecework at home or be homemakers and child tenders. This could put stress on marriages. In fact, the divorce rate in the Lower East Side was higher than in the rest of the city, and cases of desertion were common. Cahan's newspaper ran a column listing "missing men" with their photos and including pleas from their wives to contact them—much as the *Boston Pilot* did for Irish immigrants earlier in the nineteenth century.

Students may need some explanation about the wig that Gitl wears when she first arrives. Orthodox women wore a wig *(sheitel)* or a kerchief to cover their own hair as a symbol of modesty and devoutness. Orthodox men wore beards and earlocks. Jake has shaved his beard and cut his earlocks as a symbol of becoming an American and assimilating into his new culture. Gitl is upset with Jake's new demeanor and is horrified when he cuts his young son's earlocks. Jake even calls his son Yossele by a new American name, Joey, indicating a further break from the old way of life.

After 1900, economic conditions for Eastern European Jews began to improve in the United States. By the 1920s, the majority of the Jews who lived in the Lower East Side had moved to more middle-class neighborhoods in New York such as the Bronx and Brooklyn. Attempts to find compromises between the desire for Orthodox practice and the need to assimilate caused different kinds of Judaism—Conservative and Reform—to emerge. One interesting side note is that there continued to be a split (which became even wider as time went on) between German Jews, who had rapidly assimilated, and Eastern European Jews. Much of the disagreement revolved around the use of Yiddish, which the German Jews saw as backward and restrictive.

SYNOPSIS OF THE PLOT

The film opens in Joel Peltner's Dancing Academy, which has a sign proclaiming "Yiddish Spoken Here." A caption indicates that the year is 1896 and the location is the Lower East Side of New York City. Jake and Mamie meet and talk about love, marriage, and money. A new immigrant right off the boat is introduced, and Jake and his friends make fun of him, especially when he prays before taking food. Jake goes home with Mamie, who shares a room with other immigrants; their beds are separated only by sheets hung on lines.

The scene switches to the sweatshop where Jake works as a tailor. The boss makes fun of Bernstein, who was a Yeshiva (Jewish religious school) scholar in Europe and now works at a sewing machine. The boss says he was a peddler in Lithuania yet now he is the boss while the "Yeshiva boy" sweats over a sewing machine. In the Old World the situation would have been reversed, with the Yeshiva boy being revered.

Jake receives a letter from Russia telling him that his father has died. He puts on his prayer shawl and tries to pray, but cannot. When the woman he boards with is taken to the hospital, Jake rents her apartment, invites Bernstein in as a lodger to help with costs, and buys the apartment furniture. To pay for the furniture, he visits Mamie and asks to borrow money. She agrees, because she thinks that she and Jake will move in as a couple.

Jake goes to Ellis Island to meet his wife and son. The implication is that because of his father's death, they must join Jake in New York as they have no one to protect them back in Russia. Jake is astounded at how backward Gitl looks; even the immigration inspector doubts that they are husband and wife. Because she is a married woman, Gitl wears a *sheitel* or kerchief over her own hair as a symbol of devoutness and piety. Jake tells her that they don't do this in America. To further the Americanization of his family, Jake cuts off his son's earlocks so that he will look like a "Little Yankee" and changes his name from Yossele to Joey. While Gitl stays in the apartment, Jake takes Joey out into the crowded streets for a tour of his new environment.

Mamie appears at Jake's apartment and finds him with his wife and son. She is furious and demands her money back, but Jake sweet-talks her into seeing him again. Gitl tells Jake that she thought Mamie was nobility because of her dress. Jake tells Gitl to stop being such a greenhorn and to fix herself up.

A peddler comes to Gitl in the apartment with trade goods. She tries to buy a love potion to make Jake love her again. A neighbor, Mrs. Kavarsky, comes by and tells Gitl she must realize that she is not in Russia any more; she lives in an "educated country" and must dress like "educated people." Mrs. Kavarsky dresses Gitl in a corset and fancy hat. Jake does not return from work; Bernstein says that he is working late again. Bernstein teaches Joey to read Hebrew.

Jake meets Mamie at her tenement and they argue. Jake goes off to visit a prostitute. Later, in a cafe, Jake's friend Joe tells him that he is planning on marrying Mamie and using her money to run a dance academy. Ironically, Jake tells Joe that he should find a wife from the Old Country.

Gitl, Joey, Jake, and Bernstein go to the park on a picnic. Gitl wonders where the Gentiles (Christians) live in America. She has not seen any. Jake announces proudly that he is indistinguishable from a Gentile. He has lost his ethnic look and identity.

Jake arrives home from work to find that Gitl is no longer wearing a wig or kerchief and has styled her own hair. Jake becomes enraged and tells her that she looks like a "wet cat." Mrs. Kavarsky intervenes and chastises Jake for his treatment of Gitl. Gitl announces that Jake can go to Mamie and that she does not want him back. Jake meets with Mamie; she agrees to finance Jake's divorce.

Gitl meets with Mamie's lawyer, who tries to talk her into taking money for a divorce. As he keeps raising the amount, Gitl remains silent. Gitl finds Bernstein packing because he can no longer pay his board. He also has inferred that Gitl has so much money now that she does not need to have a boarder. Gitl and Bernstein talk. She agrees to become his wife, much to his surprise.

Jake arrives at a religious court to receive a *get* (divorce). Gitl arrives with Mrs. Kavarsky. It is a long ritual, and both couples must accept the divorce of their own free will. Jake has to pay all of the witnesses. Jake can get remarried immediately, but Gitl must wait 91 days. Mrs. Kavarsky tells the Rabbi's wife that Gitl is going to marry a "Yeshiva boy."

The film ends with Mamie in a wedding dress walking with Jake to City Hall to get married. Mamie tells him that since Gitl has "skinned them alive" by getting all of Mamie's money as a divorce settlement, they will have to start saving all over again. Gitl, Joey, and Bernstein are also walking down the street. They are planning the grocery store they will open using Mamie's money.

IDEAS FOR CLASS DISCUSSION

Any film involving immigration provides a good vehicle for class discussion about the reasons why various immigrant groups have left their homelands to come to America. Of all the ethnic groups arriving in the United States, Jewish immigrants arrived most often to stay, with very little remigration. Within some ethnic groups—Italians, for example—large numbers of people intended to make their money and then return to their original homeland, and many actually did so.

Another topic for discussion might be assimilation and acculturation. How much do immigrants feel the need to cast off their original culture in order to become Americans? Is it, in fact, necessary to do so? Can there be a balance between retaining some aspects of the old life and acquiring some aspects of the new homeland? Who is more likely to be happy and successful in America, Gitl or Jake? Is it more or less difficult to be an immigrant coming to the United States today?

BOOKS AND MATERIALS RELATING TO THIS FILM AND TOPIC

Carnes, Mark C. *Past Imperfect: History According to the Movies*. New York: Henry Holt and Company, 1995.

Cowan, Neil M. and Ruth Schwartz Cowan. *Our Parents' Lives: The Americanization of Eastern European Jews*. New Brunswick, NJ: Rutgers University Press, 1989.

Daniels, Roger. *Coming to America: A History of Immigration and Ethnicity in American Life*. New York: Harper Perennial, 1991.

Jones, Maldwyn A. *American Immigration*. Chicago: University of Chicago Press, 1992.

Olson, James S. *The Ethnic Dimension in American History*. 3rd ed. Naugatuck, CT: Brandywine Press, 1999.

OTHER MEDIA RESOURCES FOR THIS TIME PERIOD

Avalon (1990, 126 minutes) Movie about a Jewish family coming to the United States at the beginning of the twentieth century for a better life in the promised land.

Alamo Bay (1985, 98 minutes) A Vietnam War veteran is angered by Vietnamese immigrants who take over the fishing industry in a Texas town. Rated **R**

Far and Away (1992, 140 minutes) Directed by Ron Howard and starring Tom Cruise and Nichole Kidman, this film tells of Irish immigrants who pursue their dream first in Boston and later in the American West.

The Great Race (1965, 150 minutes) All-star cast in a comedy about an early-twentieth-century car race across three continents.

A Great Wall Is a Great Wall (1986, 97 minutes) A Chinese-American family goes to visit relatives in China and a culture clash ensues.

Joy Luck Club (1993, 139 minutes) Based on Amy Tan's book and screenplay, this film looks at four young U.S.-born Chinese-American women and their mothers, all of whom were born in China. Rated **R**

Mia Familia / My Family (1995, 128 minutes) This film examines the lives of three generations of a Hispanic family in Los Angeles, beginning with their arrival in the 1930s. Rated **R**

The Molly Maguires (1970, 123 minutes) Film about a secret society of Irish immigrant miners in 1876 Pennsylvania who fight against the cruelty of the mining companies.

Moonstruck (1987, 102 minutes) Cher stars in this comedic look at a large Italian-American family in New York.

Ragtime (1981, 155 minutes) Based on the E.L. Doctorow novel, this film, set in early-twentieth-century New York, attempts to replicate the time and setting accurately. The subplot is the notorious murder of architect Sanford White—one of the first "media events" of the twentieth century.

Rough Riders (1997, 182 minutes) Made-for-television movie about Theodore Roosevelt's band of Rough Riders and their combat in the Spanish-American War.

Thousand Pieces of Gold (1990, 105 minutes) An impoverished Chinese father sells his daughter into marriage in America in the 1880s. She runs away to a western mining town and is determined to make her way in this rough society.

UNIT 6

The Immigrant
Experience and the
Turn of the Century

HESTER STREET

Midwest Films, 1975, directed by Joan Micklin Silver

Major Character	Actor/Actress
Jake	Steven Keats
Gitl	Carol Kane
Mamie	Dorrie Kavanaugh
Mrs. Kavarsky	Doris Roberts
Yoselle (Joey)	Paul Freedman
Mr. Bernstein	Mel Howard

WHAT TO WATCH FOR

When you hear the word *immigration,* the images that usually come to mind are images from the late nineteenth and early twentieth centuries. You may picture people huddled on a ship deck looking at the Statue of Liberty, huge numbers of people in the large registry hall at Ellis Island, women in babushkas, men with long beards, wistful-looking children. Usually they are shown in clothing that is not typical of the American dress style of that era. Their "differentness" is stressed in these images.

The peak year of immigration to the United States was 1907. This last and greatest of the waves of immigration from 1890 to 1914 brought over 15 million immigrants to the country. Many of these immigrants came from southern and Eastern Europe, as opposed to earlier immigrants who came predominantly from western and northern Europe. *Hester Street* is the story of a family of Russian Jews who come to America in this last wave of immigration and how they face the challenges of their new life, particularly their assimilation into a new—and sometimes alien—culture.

(continued)

Many Jewish immigrants at the end of the nineteenth century settled initially in the Lower East Side of New York City. By 1910, half a million Jews were crowded into 1.5 square miles of the Lower East Side. Many of them lived and worked in a world where they spoke only Yiddish and communicated only with other Jews. They worked primarily in the garment industry, often at home or in sweatshops, where they were paid by the "piece." Outside of these havens, at the turn of the century there was little support for or tolerance of cultural or religious diversity. Institutions, from Ellis Island to the schools to the police and court systems, demanded assimilation into the American melting pot.

This film has a very authentic look. Note the crowded, bustling streets of the Lower East Side and how its inhabitants appear to belong to only one ethnic group. The living conditions for most immigrants in New York were very poor; Mamie shares a room with other people, and their sleeping quarters are separated by sheets hung on ropes. Privacy and open space were luxuries only for the rich. Jake has to take Bernstein in as a boarder to sleep in their combination dining room/kitchen/ living room in order to make ends meet.

Although Jews often emigrated in family groups, it was not unusual for young men to come over first, make some money, and then send for their families. Very often the husbands assimilated faster than their wives because the men were more active in the work force, although many women had to work to earn enough for their families to survive. Jake and Bernstein represent two very different versions of this adjustment to the American way of life. Note their differences in appearance, speech, and attitude.

As a devout married woman, Gitl arrives at Ellis Island with her own hair covered by a wig. You will notice that the Rabbi's wife also covers her hair. Her son has locks of hair over his ears; Orthodox Jewish men were also expected to have beards. Jake does not wish to have his ethnicity show, so he cuts his son's earlocks so that he will become a "little Yankee."

As you watch this film, notice the differences among the characters as far as their rates and degrees of assimilation. You might ask whether it is more important to retain one's Old World culture or to adapt to one's new surroundings in order to survive and thrive. Mrs. Kavarsky tells Gitl that she wears "her own hair" and that she is as pious as Gitl. She tells Gitl that America is an "educated country" and one must dress as "educated people."

Assimilation is an issue that is still a hot-button topic today. For example, should schools and businesses allow Muslims to break from their jobs or daily routine in order to pray? What if someone's traditional dress is in conflict with dress codes or requirements to wear a uniform on the job? Almost all immigrants were eager to assimilate into American culture at the turn of the twentieth century as a way of advancing themselves. At the turn of the twenty-first century, however, the value of traditional culture and language has been much more a subject for debate.

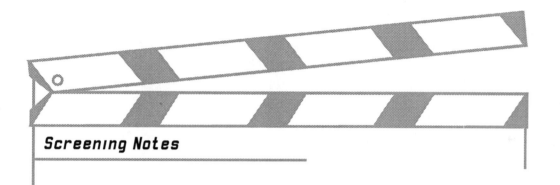

Screening Notes

The Immigrant Experience and the Turn of the Century

HESTER STREET

VOCABULARY

Ellis Island   greenhorn

Lower East Side   sweatshop

Yiddish   tenement

sheitel

QUESTIONS BASED ON THE FILM

1. How has Jake assimilated to life in America?

   _____

   _____

2. How does this film show that the Lower East Side of New York is an ethnic neighborhood?

   _____

   _____

3. As shown in the film, describe the living conditions for many immigrants in late-nineteenth-century New York.

   _____

   _____

4. What things about Gitl annoy Jake when she first arrives in America?

   _____

   _____

5. What things about Jake upset Gitl when she arrives?

    _____

    _____

    _____

6. How does Gitl change during the course of the film?

    _____

    _____

    _____

7. What things about Mamie attract Jake? Why is Gitl attracted to Mr. Bernstein?

    _____

    _____

    _____

8. How does this film present the problems of acculturation and assimilation for immigrants
    to the United States? What problems do immigrants continue to face today?

    _____

    _____

    _____

    _____

TEACHER'S GUIDE

SHOULDER ARMS

First National Pictures, 1918; directed by Charles Chaplin, black and white, silent (with musical score composed by Charles Chaplin), 40 minutes

BACKGROUND OF THE FILM

Shoulder Arms is a film that can serve a twofold purpose. First, it offers a glimpse of American attitudes during World War I; second, it provides an example of American popular culture during the era of the silent film. Furthermore, it features one of Hollywood's first major stars, Charlie Chaplin.

The story behind *Shoulder Arms* is an interesting one. Although he lived largely in the United States and was a prominent cultural icon there, Charlie Chaplin was a British citizen. After the beginning of World War I, Englishmen who did not enlist were subjected to humiliation and scathing attacks. White feathers were sometimes sent to them as symbols of cowardice, and Chaplin received his share—as well as being attacked publicly in the press. The main reason why Chaplin was actually left alone by the British government was not only because his wealth allowed him to contribute to Britain's war funds, but also because he fostered immense sympathy in the U.S. for the British cause. This was important since American economic assistance was increasingly necessary for the Allied war effort.

In 1917, when Chaplin signed a contract with First National for $1 million, with a signing bonus of $15,000, the campaign in the press against him increased in viciousness. By this time, the United States had entered the war. It was reported that Chaplin went to an army recruiting office but was rejected for being underweight. News of this did cause the campaign against him to diminish.

Chaplin then put his energies into campaigning for Liberty Bonds to finance the American war effort. Early in 1918, he produced a short film called *The Bond* (also available on video), which features Charlie hitting the Kaiser on the head with a huge hammer emblazoned with the words *Liberty Bonds*.

It is against this historical background that Chaplin wrote, directed, and starred in *Shoulder Arms,* which was released only a matter of months before the armistice. The film was originally planned as a "five reeler," although it was later released in three reels. (Films were advertised based on the number of reels—each reel anywhere from 12 to 14 minutes long—rather than running time.) At a time when most studios' output was dominated by vicious anti-German propaganda, Chaplin went ahead with the film against the advice of many in the movie industry, who felt that World War I was not a topic for laughter and jest.

The failure of the German offensive in spring 1918, and the subsequent turning of the tide of war to the Allies' side that summer, made the topic of the film more palatable. The film was, in fact, a huge box-office success. Cutout figures of Charlie that had adorned the entrances of movie theaters were carried off overseas by soldiers and set up on the parapets of trenches during enemy attacks. This totally confused the Germans, who did not know who Chaplin was. Chaplin's familiarity as a cultural icon was also used to treat shell-shocked soldiers. A photo of Charlie was sometimes shown to these soldiers with the hope of distracting them and eliciting a response.

Many of the gags in *Shoulder Arms* are dated, because Chaplin used topics that were in the wartime public's mind. Cooties (lice), packages from home, the telegrapher in no-man's-land, the flooded dugout, the primitive camouflage, stereotypical spiky-mustached and fat Germans, threadbare France as a heroine at the mercy of barbarian hordes, and the dream of a breakout and heroic climax to the war were, though exaggerated by Chaplin, true wartime realities and desires. The film contains what we would call sight gags and stage humor, but in the center was Chaplin himself, the beloved clown. If he had been any less a pitiable Everyman, he would not have been the object of the viewer's laughter and delight. *Shoulder Arms* gave audiences in America and Europe a bit of reality-based humor during an otherwise grim and humorless time.

The silent film is an art form that many of your students may not have seen before. Although sound had been experimented with by Thomas Edison as early as the first decade of the 1900s, it was not commercially viable until the late 1920s. Without having to synchronize sound, silent films were usually shot at the rate of 16–18 frames per second but were projected at 20–24 frames per second. This meant that the tempo was much quicker and the movements of individuals lighter and more ethereal than in real life.

This pace is what gave Chaplin's movements their unique dancelike quality and his characteristic walk its jerkiness. There were "billboards" (intertitles) clarifying the story, but most of the "narration" had to be projected by the actors' gestures and facial expressions. A musical score accompanying the film (for many of Chaplin's films these were composed by Chaplin himself) was usually played on a piano or organ in the theater. Because of the flammability of silver nitrate film, the practice of recycling film to extract the silver, or just plain neglect, the majority of silent films are now gone. *Shoulder Arms* can give students a chance to experience this type of film art.

SYNOPSIS OF THE PLOT

The film opens with Charlie's hand signing his name and pointing at a picture of himself. Charlie is then shown as an army recruit who gets just about everything wrong. He turns the wrong way and cannot get his feet to stop turning out at a nearly impossible angle.

Charlie arrives in a trench on the front carrying an impossible amount of equipment, including his own mousetrap and a cheese grater to use as a back scratcher. His bedroll is number 13. When the enemy soldiers appear, they are weirdly shaped and sized, with spiky mustaches and pointed German helmets. Shells explode near Charlie, and his helmet flips up in the air each time one lands. He dreams of life in the city, where he can be a bartender making cocktails—something to which real soldiers could certainly relate after months in the trenches.

Packages arrive from home, but Charlie doesn't get one. While others eat their goodies sent from home, Charlie eats the cheese from his mousetrap and reads a letter over the shoulder of another soldier. When a package does arrive for Charlie, it contains dog biscuits and Limburger cheese, a common subject for jokes in silent films. Charlie lobs the cheese into the enemy lines, where it hits a German officer in the face.

In the dugout, which is totally flooded, Charlie fluffs his pillow and tries to sleep nearly submerged in water. When he wakes up, he can't feel his foot; it turns out that the foot he has been rubbing doesn't belong to him.

The order comes: "Over the top." After a few mishaps with ladders, Charlie succeeds and is able to capture a German trench. Charlie offers cigarettes to his captives, then marches them off.

The billboard reads "Poor France," and the scene switches to a French girl sitting dejectedly on the front step of her destroyed house. Meanwhile, Charlie and his buddy (played by his brother Syd) are sitting in the trench eating. Note how Charlie gets his bottle open and cigarette lit.

Volunteers are called for. Charlie ends up being a volunteer camouflaged as a tree behind enemy lines. When a German tries to cut him down, Charlie knocks him out—as well as two others who come along. His comrade is captured by the Germans and is about to be shot when "Charlie the tree" intervenes. He is chased into a forest by a rather fat German who has trouble finding him. Charlie escapes by crawling into a culvert and eventually arriving at the destroyed French home. When the French girl arrives, she finds Charlie asleep. Through sign language, he is able to reassure her that he is an American soldier. When the Germans come looking for him, she helps him escape.

The French girl is arrested by the Germans and left alone with a leering officer. Charlie comes down the chimney and rescues her by pushing the German into a closet. When the kaiser himself arrives at the front, Charlie hides in the closet also.

When the kaiser demands to see the officer, Charlie emerges from the closet dressed in a German uniform, and he struts around arrogantly. His comrade has been captured again, and Charlie pretends to rough him up. However, the kaiser's chauffeur suspects something. Charlie and his comrade capture the chauffeur while the kaiser, von Hindenberg, and the crown prince are getting drunk. Charlie and the French girl dress like the chauffeur and his assistant; then the kaiser gets into the car. The comrade sends word to the Allies that Charlie has captured the kaiser, and he drives into the middle of the American camp to cheers.

In the next scene, Charlie is on his cot in his tent at training camp. He has dreamed the entire thing.

IDEAS FOR CLASS DISCUSSION

When discussing this film in class, have students think about what a soldier mired in the trenches of World War I would find humorous. Obviously, the flooded dugouts, packages from home, Charlie trying to march correctly, and the ever-present cooties would mostly likely ring true. It also is essential to discuss how important Charlie Chaplin was as an

iconic figure. He was the first real American cinema megastar, and his films were viewed as morale boosters.

The stereotypes inherent in the film also would be a good topic for discussion—the fat Germans with their impossibly pointed mustaches and the characterization of France as a poor, desolate, and defenseless female who needs the help of an American soldier in order to persevere. This film was produced late in the war; therefore, the Germans are portrayed more comically than they might have been earlier, when an Allied victory was less assured.

How would the sudden and happy ending of the film appeal to nations who had been embroiled in several years of conflict? The silent film as a common American art form of the early twentieth century could also be a topic for class discussion.

BOOKS AND MATERIALS RELATING TO THIS FILM AND TOPIC

Brownlow, Kevin. *The War, the West, and the Wilderness.* New York: Alfred A. Knopf, 1979.

Campbell, Craig W. *Reel America and World War I: A Comprehensive Filmography and History of Motion Pictures in the United States, 1914–1920.* Jefferson, NC: MacFarland, 1985.

Collier, Richard. *The Plague of the Spanish Lady: The Influenza Pandemic of 1918–1919.* New York: Atheneum, 1974.

Devlin, Patrick. *Too Proud to Fight: Woodrow Wilson's Neutrality.* New York: Oxford University Press, 1975.

Ellis, Edward Robb. *Echoes of Distant Thunder: Life in the United States, 1914–1918.* New York: Coward, McCann, and Geoghegan, 1975.

Isenberg, Michael. *War on Film: The American Cinema and World War I, 1914–1941.* Rutherford, NJ: Fairleigh Dickinson University Press, 1981.

Kerr, Walter. *The Silent Clowns.* New York: Alfred A. Knopf, 1975.

Rollins, Peter C., and John E. O'Connor, eds. *Holly-wood's World War I: Motion Picture Images.* Bowling Green, OH: Bowling Green State University Popular Press, 1997.

OTHER MEDIA RESOURCES FOR THIS TIME PERIOD

Feature Films

The Big Parade (1925, 126 minutes) King Vidor's silent antiwar epic, based on the story of Laurence Stallings, who served as a marine in the war and lost his leg (as does the movie's hero, played by John Gilbert) at Belleau Wood

The Cardinal (1963, 175 minutes) Otto Preminger's film based on Henry Morton Robinson's reverential novel about the trials and growth of an American priest in the context of war, racial and religious bigotry, and the rise of European fascism

Civilization (1916, 102 minutes) Thomas Ince's morality play about the immorality of war; produced while America was still neutral in the World War I, it boosted the appeal of Woodrow Wilson as a presidential candidate, since he "kept us out of war." It is a silent-era film with printed intertexts and a musical score.

A Farewell to Arms (1932, 78 minutes) Gary Cooper and Helen Hayes starred in this version of Hemingway's semiautobiographical novel. An inferior remake appeared in 1957.

Hearts of the World (1918, 122 minutes) The film made by D. W. Griffith at the request of the British government. Griffith got permission to film near the front in France and brought his stars, Lillian and Dorothy Gish, to shoot scenes there. The resulting footage, however, was not visually exciting enough for American moviegoers. Griffith and his crew then retreated to southwestern England, where the British Army (though desperately short of ammunition) helped him to create the kind of war scenes Americans expected—with exciting, romantic battles and with clear heroes and villains.

This film is silent, with intercards and a musical score.

In Love and War (1996, 113 minutes) Story of reporter and writer Ernest Hemingway, who worked as an ambulance driver during World War I

Johnny Got His Gun (1971, 111 minutes) A depressing film made during the Vietnam War era by once-blacklisted Dalton Trumbo from his 1939 antiwar novel. Timothy Bottoms plays an American soldier who has lost his arms, legs, and communication faculties to a German artillery shell. He now silently remembers his life from the living tomb of his hospitalized body. Rated **R**

The Lost Battalion (2001, 100 minutes) Describes the events experienced by the U.S. Army's 77th Division, 308th Battalion, which was surrounded by German troops in the Argonne Forest in October 1918

1918 (1985, 89 minutes) Based upon a Horton Foote play, this gem is about the impact of World War I on a small Texas town. Hard to find, but sometimes available as a used copy

Reds (1981, 200 minutes) Warren Beatty's biographical film about American radical journalist John Reed and his relationship with Louise Bryant; the film carries us through the tumultuous years of the First World War, the Russian and Bolshevik revolutions, the birth pangs of the American Communist party, and the Russian Civil War, in which Reed died.

Sergeant York (1940, 134 minutes) The film biography of the World War I Congressional Medal of Honor winner who captured 132 German soldiers almost single-handedly; telling the story as a pacifist-turned-soldier must be seen as part of the "preparedness" movement that was growing in the United States in 1940.

Wilson (1944, 154 minutes) Made during World War II, this film portrays the World War I president as an idealist thwarted by shortsighted politicians as he obsessively pursues his vision of a new world order embodied in the League of Nations. The film was meant to be a salutary lesson to Americans preparing to remake the world near the end of an even more destructive war.

Wings (1927, 139 minutes) The other silent film classic about the war, this time about the air war; despite the sound revolution that was taking Hollywood by storm when this film was made, it was *Wings* that won the first Best Picture award.

Documentaries

Goodbye Billy: America Goes to War, 1917–1918 (1972, 25 minutes) A film made by three historians in association with the American Historical Association's History Education Project

The Great War (1956, 54 minutes) One of the classic NBC *Project XX* documentaries

The Great War—1918 (1989, 57 minutes) Part of the PBS *American Experience* series

Hollywood Goes to War (1980, 54 minutes) This film is Kevin Brownlow and David Gill's *Hollywood: The Silent Years* episode about World War I's impact on Hollywood.

Homefront 1917-1919: War Transforms American Life (1967, 17 minutes) Briefly covers American wartime life and attitudes

Men of Bronze (1977, 57 minutes) The story of the U.S. Army's 369th Infantry Regiment—the unit of African Americans that served longer in action than any other American unit

The Moving Picture Boys in the Great War (1986, 52 minutes) is a documentary about the newsreels narrated by Lowell Thomas.

The Yanks Are Coming (1974, 52 minutes) David Wolper's documentary about America's role in the war

SHOULDER ARMS

First National Pictures, 1918; directed by Charles Chaplin

Major Character	Actor/Actress
Recruit	Charles Chaplin
Sergeant, the Kaiser	Syd Chaplin
French girl	Edna Purviance
German crown prince	Jack Wilson
German sergeant, von Hindenberg	Henry Bergman
American soldier, german soldier,	
Kaiser's chauffeur	Albert Austin
Training camp sergeant	Tom Wilson
Short German officer	Loyal Underwood

WHAT TO WATCH FOR

This silent film was released about two months before the end of World War I. The writer, director, and star, Charles Chaplin, was nervous about making a film that portrayed the war in a humorous way. However, the ability of the Allies to meet a German offensive in the summer of 1918, and prospects for an Allied victory in the fall of 1918, made this film more palatable to American and British audiences. In fact, *Shoulder Arms* was a huge box-office success, building upon the great popularity of Charlie Chaplin, one of Hollywood's first megastars.

Note how Chaplin satirizes the life of an average soldier in the war, from basic training to life in the trenches. Some images might seem strange to you—learning to march correctly, the flooded dugout, the ever-present "cooties" (cooties are lice—note the use of a cheese grater as a back scratcher), the packages from home containing goodies, and the names for the trenches such as Broadway and Rotten Row. However, these were common to audiences at the time, particularly to

(continued)

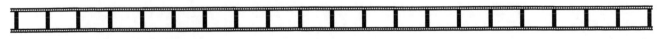

soldiers, who loved the movie. Soldiers actually sang a song in the trenches called "The moon shines bright on Charlie Chaplin." American soldiers even stole cardboard cutouts of Chaplin that had been used to decorate the entrances to movie theaters and hoisted them onto the top of trench walls at the front. This totally bewildered the Germans, most of whom didn't know who Chaplin was.

How would this film appeal to an audience whose country had been mired in a war of attrition for four long years, as was the case for the British? Think of how the film would have appealed to Americans, who felt that their intervention was the crucial turning point for the Allies. The "dream" victory of the film contrasted sharply with the reality of the times, but most filmgoers did not wish to see a slice of reality; they wanted to be entertained and offered an escape.

Silent films were very popular from the turn of the century until the beginning of sound in the late 1920s. Because there was no need to synchronize with sound, films could be shot at one or several speeds, then shown either sped up or slowed down. The quick chase scenes and the jerky motions of the actors are the result of this inconsistency in film speed and real life. Billboards and the actors' gestures, as well as the music, which was played live while the film was being shown, helped to get the message across. For this reason, silent films are not subtle; there is quite a bit of what we would call slapstick or stage humor in silent-era comedies.

Screening Notes

──────── *SHOULDER ARMS* ────────────────────

VOCABULARY

camouflage   the Great War
cooties   Kaiser
dugout   trench warfare
the front

QUESTIONS BASED ON THE FILM

1. Which aspects of military life, both on the home front during training and at the front itself, does Chaplin satirize in this film?

   _____

   _____

   _____

   _____

2. How does Chaplin let his audience know that he is just an "ordinary" American in the film? What are the characteristics of the ordinary American soldiers shown?

   _____

   _____

   _____

   _____

3. How is the enemy portrayed? Contrast the way the enemy is shown in this film, made late in the war, with earlier American portrayals of the enemy in such things as poster art.

_____

_____

_____

4. How is France portrayed in this film?

_____

_____

_____

5. How is heroism and its role in the war dealt with?

_____

_____

_____

6. Why was Chaplin worried about making this sort of film? Were these fears justified?

_____

_____

_____

7. What "lesson" does this film teach? What do you think an American audience viewing this film in the closing months of the war would believe about America's role in the war?

_____

_____

_____

_____

TEACHER'S GUIDE

MATEWAN

Cinecom Entertainment Group and Film Gallery, 1987; directed by John Sayles, color, 100 minutes

BACKGROUND OF THE FILM

Matewan was both written and directed by John Sayles. It was produced as a low-budget (under $5 million) film independent of any major studio. Despite the drawbacks in trying to "sell" a movie that had an intensely political theme, no rock music, and no upbeat ending, and the problems involved in producing a low-budget movie set in the past and therefore requiring authentic sets and costumes, *Matewan* was a critical success.

Sayles first became interested in writing *Matewan* while hitchhiking through the coal-mining areas of Kentucky and West Virginia. In 1977, he wrote a novel called *Union Dues*. During the course of the research for that book, he came across references to the "Matewan massacre" and to a chief of police in Matewan, West Virginia, named Sid Hatfield, a distant cousin of the Hatfields involved in the legendary feud with the McCoys.

The history of the 1920 Matewan massacre revolves around the efforts of the United Mine Workers (UMW) to unionize the coal fields of eastern Kentucky and southwestern West Virginia. The United Mine Workers targeted Logan and Mingo Counties to be organized and sent agents into these areas. The mine owners, who had been able to undercut the unionized mines to the north by paying lower wages, were anxious to stop the UMW, an organization that they saw as a creeping disease. Nationwide, public opinion tended to side with the mine operators since, during the Red scare that followed World War I, unions were often equated with the "Bolshevik menace." A strike broke out in Matewan, on the Tug Fort River near the Kentucky border. The mayor of the town, Cabell Testerman, and chief of police, Sid Hatfield, sided with the miners and refused to be bought by the coal company. When agents from the Baldwin-Felts Detective Agency, working for the coal operators, came to evict the miners from company housing, Hatfield confronted them. Shots were fired and, in the ensuing massacre, seven Baldwin-Felts agents, Mayor Testerman, and two miners were killed.

From this basic history, John Sayles fleshed out the story of *Matewan,* using the real characters of Testerman and Hatfield and adding other real, fictional, or composite characters from his research on this period. Few Clothes was a real person, as was the skilled company spy, C.E. Lively. Two main fictional characters are the chief protagonist, the union organizer Joe Kenehan, and the young miner and preacher Danny Radnor. The movie is framed by a narration, which is spoken by Danny as an old man, although we never see him. Sayles decided to focus his movie on the role and effects of violence and, to this end, he made Joe a pacifist. To make him a believable character, Sayles made him a "Wobbly"—a member of the Industrial Workers of the World (IWW), an American union aimed at organizing whole industries rather than individual skilled crafts, which was the focus of the contemporary American Federation of Labor (AF of L). Historically the IWW, with its promise of uniting all workers into one big union and then using

65

general strikes to achieve its objectives, was considered much more of a threat to the American system of business and industry than the AF of L. When the IWW opposed American participation in World War I, government, industry, and the AF of L combined to hound it nearly to extinction. The IWW form of industrywide organizing reemerged in the philosophy of the Congress of Industrial Organizations (CIO) in which the United Mine Workers played a founding role. Danny becomes a convert to Joe's crusade, and afterward he carries on Joe's work.

Many elements of the story are based on fact. Following a long tradition, the coal companies did bring in Italian immigrants and Southern blacks as strikebreakers. The company did own the miners' houses as well as the churches, stores, and just about everything else in the mining towns, and it could evict miners without notice or any right of legal redress. Striking miners were forced to set up tent camps after they were evicted from their housing. The references throughout the movie to the union and its organizers as "Reds," "Bolsheviks," or "Communists" are indicative of a time when Red-baiting was effective propaganda for convincing Americans that unions were dangerous and un-American.

SYNOPSIS OF THE PLOT

A narrator sets the time and place—1920 in Matewan, West Virginia. As coal miners learn that the mine operators have brought down the tonnage rate for coal, thereby lowering their wages, they go out on strike. The coal operators bring in black men from Alabama as strikebreakers on the same train to Matewan as Joe Kenehan, an agent sent by the union to organize the miners.

Joe rents a room at Elma Radnor's house; there he meets her son Danny, a trapper boy in the mine and a preacher. Joe is brought to a meeting of the miners at C.E. Lively's Restaurant. The unofficial leader of the black strikebreakers, Few Clothes Johnson, comes to the meeting to make it clear that he is not a scab. Joe urges all the miners to walk out and states that anyone

who does will be brought into the union regardless of color or national origin.

In response to the strike, the coal operators send two Baldwin-Felts agents, Hickey and Griggs, into town to evict the miners from company housing. Police Chief Sid Hatfield prevents the evictions and deputizes the miners.

When the miners go to confront the black and Italian strikebreakers, the blacks, led by Few Clothes, and the Italians, led by Fausto, throw down their shovels and join the strike. They are welcomed into the union, and blacks and whites work together to build a tent camp, since they cannot live in the company housing.

Still in town, the Baldwin-Felts agents try to bribe Sid and the mayor to cooperate. The tent camp is attacked at night and there is a shoot-out between the miners and the coal company guards. One miner is killed and the audience learns that C.E. is a company spy.

To break the miners' trust in Joe, C.E. coerces a young townswoman, Bridey Mae, to say Joe raped her, and C.E. tries to show that Joe is a collaborator with the Baldwin-Felts agents. The miners draw straws and Few Clothes is picked to kill Joe. Danny overhears Hickey and Griggs discussing Joe's fate; he preaches a sermon that tells the miners of this treachery. Jace Hilliard, a young mine worker, reaches Few Clothes in time to save Joe's life. The union pulls together once more, and Joe is seen doling out strike-relief money.

C.E. tells Turley, the mine manager, that he would like to bring things to a boil. Hilliard is caught stealing coal. Griggs slits his throat on a command from C.E., who then proclaims, "Nothin' like a young boy dyin' to stir things up."

The next day the train brings in a group of Baldwin-Felts men to try once more to carry out evictions in the town. Sid confronts them. A shoot-out takes place between the Baldwin-Felts men, Sid, and the miners. The Felts brothers, Hickey, Griggs, the mayor, and Joe Kenehan are killed.

The narration of the old man comes back in to finish the story. In the last scene, we see a lone miner who is shown to be Danny. We realize that the narrator is Danny as an old man, who has pledged himself to carry on Joe's mission.

IDEAS FOR CLASS DISCUSSION

Labor unions in the United States today are often characterized as bloated, corrupt, and bureaucratic special interests. By opening this window to the post-World War I period of labor-management relations, students can explore the nature of industrial and extraction enterprise, the traditional ways in which management exerted control over labor, and the reasons why workers turned to collective bargaining to redress the balance. In the process, the class can discuss the role of government in the economic sector, the alternative modes of labor union organization, the use of political or ideological labels to mark economic self-interest, the ways in which racial and ethnic differences intersected with class interests and were used to prevent unionization, and the role violence played in labor history.

BOOKS AND MATERIALS
RELATING TO THIS FILM AND TOPIC

Burns, James MacGregor. *The Workshop of Democracy.* New York: Alfred A. Knopf, 1985.

Carter, Paul Allen. *Another Part of the Twenties.* New York: Columbia University Press, 1977.

Long, Priscilla. *Where the Sun Never Shines: A History of America's Bloody Coal Industry.* New York: Paragon House, 1989.

Phillips, Cabell. "The West Virginia Mine War." *American Heritage* 25, no. 5 (August 1974): 58–61.

Sayles, John. *Thinking in Pictures: The Making of the Movie* Matewan. Boston: Houghton-Mifflin, 1987.

OTHER MEDIA RESOURCES
FOR THIS TIME PERIOD

The Court Martial of Billy Mitchell (1955, 100 minutes) Deals with the struggle over military preparedness and the role of air power during the traditionalist and isolationist mood of the 1920s

Eight Men Out (1988, 119 minutes) A John Sayles film about the 1919 Chicago "Black Sox" baseball scandal

The Great Gatsby (1974, 146 minutes) A look at the well-to-do of the Roaring Twenties through the eyes of its greatest literary character, F. Scott Fitzgerald

Inherit the Wind (1960, 127 minutes) The film version of the Jerome Lawrence/Robert E. Lee play about the 1925 Scopes "Monkey Trial" that pitted evolutionary theory against the authority of the Bible, and Clarence Darrow (Spencer Tracy) against William Jennings Bryan (Fredric March)

Rosewood (1997, 140 minutes) True story of how the African-American community of Rosewood, Florida, was burned and its citizens murdered in 1923; rated **R**

Sacco and Vanzetti (1971, 120 minutes) An Italian film with English dubbed in that investigates the 1921 trial and eventual execution of the two Italian immigrants on charges of robbery and murder—charges that many believe resulted from their anarchist politics rather than their guilt

The Spirit of St. Louis (1957, 137 minutes) The story of America's greatest hero, Charles A. Lindbergh, in a decade that exalted heroes

MATEWAN

Cinecom Entertainment Group and Film Gallery, 1987; directed by John Sayles

Major Character	Actor/Actress
Joe Kenehan	Chris Cooper
Few Clothes Johnson	James Earl Jones
Danny Radnor	Will Oldham
Elma Radnor	Mary McDonnell
Sid Hatfield	David Strathairn
C.E. Lively	Bob Gunton
Bridey Mae	Nancy Mette
Hilliard Elkins	Jace Alexander
Hickey	Kevin Tighe
Griggs	Gordon Clapp
Cabell Testerman	Josh Mostel

WHAT TO WATCH FOR

This film is based on a true event: the so-called "Matewan massacre" of 1920. This was a shoot-out between gunmen of the Baldwin-Felts Detective Agency, working for mine owners, and striking miners. The police chief, Sid Hatfield, and the mayor of Matewan, Cabell Testerman, sided with the miners—an unusual occurrence at a time when mining towns were owned and controlled by the coal operators.

In most historical films, the events and characters are "telescoped"; the time span is cut down and the number of characters reduced to make the story easier to comprehend. Sayles, however, has added characters and stretched events out. His two main characters, union organizer Joe Kenehan, and young miner Danny Radnor, are fictional characters, added to help tell a story. Joe and Danny *could* have existed; they conform to the attitudes and personalities of that time and place. Few Clothes

(continued)

Johnson, the leader of the black miners brought in as strikebreakers, was a real person whom Sayles discovered while researching the topic of Matewan.

The unionization of the coalfields of eastern Kentucky and southwestern West Virginia was a bloody chapter in U.S. labor history. This movie portrays many of the issues of that struggle. Note how the coal companies exert economic control over the miners, as in the scene where the mine manager is going over company rules and so-called "benefits" with the newly hired black miners. Note also the popular prejudices against unions and union activities as expressed by the hard-shell preacher and the Baldwin-Felts agents. Popular opinion in the United States was on the side of the coal operators, who wanted to prevent the United Mine Workers union from entering the coalfields.

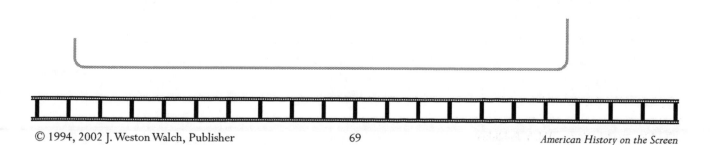

Screening Notes

UNIT 8

The Twenties

———— *MATEWAN* ————

VOCABULARY

Bolshevik

Wobblies

scab

UMW

company store

QUESTIONS BASED ON THE FILM

1. What are the miners' complaints against the mine owners that have led them to go on strike?

_____

_____

_____

_____

2. How does the coal operator in Matewan exert an economic hold on the miners? (*Hint:* Think of the scene where Turley explains company policies to the newly hired black miners.)

_____

_____

_____

_____

(continued)

3. What is the role of music in the film? How is it used to set the mood or tell a story?

   _____

   _____

   _____

   _____

4. Why is there, on the part of so many, a suspicion against unions during this time in American history?

   _____

   _____

   _____

   _____

5. After Hilliard's death, what are Danny's arguments against Joe's pacificism and the union?

   _____

   _____

   _____

   _____

The Great Depression

TEACHER'S GUIDE

THE GRAPES OF WRATH

Twentieth Century-Fox, 1940; directed by John Ford, black and white, 129 minutes; John Ford won an Academy Award® for Best Director. Jane Darwell won an Oscar® for Best Supporting Actress.

BACKGROUND OF THE FILM

The Great Depression was one of the most devastating events in American history, and nowhere was the impact more poignant than among the small farmers of the Great Plains. Overfarming, poor land use, depressed agricultural prices, absentee landlords, and long-term drought had caused the south central states to become the Dust Bowl. Thousands of sharecroppers and small farmers (known as "Okies" or "Arkies," depending on their home state) were thrown off or blown off the land with virtually nowhere to go. Many were lured to California by the promise of agricultural jobs in the rich valleys of the "Golden State."

John Steinbeck's Pulitzer Prize-winning novel about a family of sharecroppers from Oklahoma trying to find work and stay together as a family unit became an immediate classic. Darryl F. Zanuck of Twentieth Century-Fox bought the movie rights to the book for $75,000—the highest price paid for any novel of the 1930s, even exceeding the amount paid for *Gone With the Wind.* The movie almost immediately became the subject of much controversy. At first Zanuck was accused of delaying production of the movie because of pressure from business and agricultural interests and Oklahoma and California state

officials. When shooting did begin, Zanuck was accused of softening the desolate picture Steinbeck had portrayed of the migrant Okies. Then, when the film was finally shown to be sensitive to the tragic plight of the migrants, mainstream critics objected to the picture—or any picture—having such a bleak message and not providing pure entertainment. Others, particularly some on the left, objected to the glossing over of the economic sources of the evil. One critic, Ernest L. Mayers, did defend Zanuck, pointing out that if there could not be films with a message, that would only leave room for mysteries, fairy tales, thin men, and the two Mickeys—Rooney and Mouse. (David Zinman, *Fifty Classic Motion Pictures.* Chelsea House, 1983, p. 190.)

Ultimately, the film was a commercial success; however, even though it has come to be regarded as a film classic, it remains controversial in many ways. Many critics continue to feel that Ford changed the radical political and economic nature of Steinbeck's novel into a more politically conservative story in which the major emphasis is on the strength and perseverance of the American family. Instead of images that reflect the land and the social conditions of the time, most of the visual images revolve around the Joad family. Most of the film was shot indoors or on a studio lot, with many views of the Joads and other Okies taking on the appearance of tableaus that reflected popular iconography of the Great Depression as seen in the photographs of Walker Evans or Dorothea Lange. Teachers might wish to use these photos with this film as a good supplementary source.

SYNOPSIS OF THE PLOT

The movie begins with a graphic explaining the Dust Bowl and the statement that this is the story of one family's experience. The scene then opens with Tom Joad walking along a country road in Oklahoma. He has just been paroled from the penitentiary after serving four years for homicide. On his way to the family home he meets Casy, a preacher, who tells him that there is much to preach about now. Tom finds his family home deserted. He meets Muley, a sharecropper like himself, who tells Tom that his family is at Uncle John's house and that everyone is being forced off the land. The Caterpillar™ tractor has replaced the sharecropper; one tractor can do the work of 14 farmers. Tom finds his family preparing to leave for California, where a handbill has advertised good pay for 800 fruit pickers. The family of 12 loads up the old Hudson truck and heads west on Route 66 with their life savings of $150.

The trip is too much for the old people; Grampa suffers a stroke and dies. He is buried by the roadside, where Tom leaves a note saying: "This here is Willeam James Joad, dyed of a stroke, old, old man. His folks buried him because they got no money to pay for funerals. Nobody killed him, just a stroke and he dyed." When the family stops for the night at a camp, they meet a man who has been to California. He warns them that there are no jobs. Granma dies during the desert crossing, but Ma pretends that Granma is merely sick in order to get quickly through the agricultural inspectors at the California border.

The Joads arrive at a camp crowded with Okies all looking for work. As Ma is cooking, she is surrounded by dozens of starving children. A work contractor comes to the camp to recruit workers, but he won't say what the wage is. A fight breaks out and a deputy kills a woman bystander. Tom trips the deputy before he can fire again; he then flees to avoid capture. Casy is taken away as an agitator. The Joad family flees the camp upon learning that people from a nearby town are planning to burn it down.

The Joads get a job at the Keene Ranch picking peaches for five cents a box. The conditions are poor and the ranch is surrounded by angry workers. Tom meets Casy who tells him that some workers are on strike. He urges Tom to come out and join the protestors to keep the price up. While they are meeting, a group of guards attacks and kills Casy. Tom kills a guard and is marked across the face. The Joad family escapes the farm at night while hiding Tom.

The family finally checks into a camp run by the Department of Agriculture. The camp is run democratically by the workers themselves and the conditions are dramatically different from the previous camp. Still, there is hostility toward the Okies, and the camp is warned that there will be trouble at the Saturday night dance. Deputies move in, but the camp members have defused any problems. Later that night, Tom wakes to hear two policemen checking his license number; he realizes that they are on his trail. Tom knows that to protect his family, he must leave. In his farewell to Ma, Tom vows to carry on Casy's fight.

The Joads hear of work in Fresno and push on, always hoping for something better. Ma keeps them together; the film ends with her exclamation: "We're the people that live. Can't wipe us out. Can't lick us. We'll go on forever. 'Cause we're the people."

IDEAS FOR CLASS DISCUSSION

Of course, to read Steinbeck's novel would be an ideal way to approach this film. How faithful is the film to the original mood and story line of the book? The farmers of the Dust Bowl present an indelible image of the Great Depression for many Americans, but what were the experiences of people in other parts of the country? It is strongly recommended that teachers show the short documentary *The Plow That Broke the Plains* in conjunction with the showing of *The Grapes of Wrath*.

BOOKS AND MATERIALS RELATING TO THIS FILM AND TOPIC

Bonnifield, Paul. *The Dust Bowl: Men, Dirt and the Depression.* Albuquerque: University of New Mexico Press, 1979.

French, Warren G. *Filmguide to* The Grapes of Wrath. Bloomington, IN: Indiana University Press, 1973.

Hurt, Douglas. *The Dust Bowl: An Agricultural and Social History: American Film in a Cultural Context.* Chicago: Nelson Hall, 1981.

Rollins, Peter C., ed. *Hollywood as Historian.* Lexington, KY: University Press of Kentucky, 1983.

Steinbeck, John. *The Grapes of Wrath.* New York: The Viking Press, 1939.

Zinman, David. *Fifty Classic Motion Pictures: The Stuff That Dreams Are Made Of.* New York: Limelight Editions, 1992.

OTHER MEDIA RESOURCES FOR THIS TIME PERIOD

Bonnie and Clyde (1967, 111 minutes) The story of a group of bank robbers who terrorized the Midwest in the 1930s and became tragic folk heroes; note that the choreographed violence in the film is quite graphic, especially at the end.

The Color Purple (1985, 152 minutes) Starring Whoopie Goldberg, this film is about black survival in the Depression-era South.

Cradle Will Rock (1999, 134 minutes) Orson Welles and a troupe of actors attempt to put on a controversial play. Good slice-of-life look at Depression-era New York City. Rated **R**

Eleanor and Franklin (1976, 208 minutes) Story of President Roosevelt and his wife from their youth to FDR's death in 1945 as told from Eleanor's point of view

Hoodlum (1997, 130 minutes) Two rival gangs in 1930s Harlem fight it out for control of illegal gaming.

Oh Brother, Where Art Thou? (2000, 106 minutes) Coen Brothers' film that presents a slice of life during the 1930s; convicts escape and try to reach some loot from a bank robbery that they have hidden in a house; great soundtrack of Depression-era music.

Our Daily Bread (1934, 71 minutes) A classic dealing with the effects of the Depression and the attempt of some displaced urbanites to "return to the land" and start an agricultural cooperative

Places in the Heart (1984, 102 minutes) A film about agricultural survival and social tolerance in Waxahachie, Texas, during the Depression

The Plow That Broke the Plains (1936, 26 minutes) Pare Lorentz's classic documentary sponsored by the New Deal's Resettlement Administration; a version that restores the film's original ending, which advertised New Deal agencies and caused a furor in Congress, along with a frame-by-frame commentary and a set of source materials related to the film, is available as part of the *Image As Artifact* video package from the American Historical Association.

Radio Days (1987, 96 minutes) Woody Allen movie sentimentalizing the Golden Age of radio

RKO 281 (1999, 87 minutes) A feature film based upon a PBS documentary about Orson Welles and William Randolph Hearst; rated **R**

Roll of Thunder, Hear my Cry (1978, 95 minutes) Morgan Freeman stars in a drama of a black family's struggle to survive during the Great Depression in the American South. Unlike the book, the video is confusing and disjointed.

The Sting (1973, 129 minutes) Paul Newman film that reflects the mood of Depression-era America.

To Kill a Mockingbird (1963, 129 minutes) The classic story of a six-year-old growing up in a small Southern town and confronting racial bigotry

THE GRAPES OF WRATH

Twentieth Century-Fox, 1940; directed by John Ford

Major Character	Actor/Actress
Tom Joad	Henry Fonda
Ma Joad	Jane Darwell
Casy	John Carradine
Pa Joad	Russell Simpson
Grampa	Charley Grapewin
Granma	Zeffie Tilbury
Muley	John Qualen

WHAT TO WATCH FOR

Based on John Steinbeck's Pulitzer Prize-winning novel of 1939, this film has become a classic in its own right.

The Great Depression was a devastating event in twentieth-century America. This film chronicles its effect on the Joad family of Oklahoma. Poor farming practices and an extended drought turned the south central states into the Dust Bowl. Lured by the promise of jobs and good pay, thousands of "Okies," like the Joads, loaded up their jalopies and made the trek to California. What they find in the "Promised Land" is that the surplus of labor and shortage of jobs has led the growers to slash wages to near-starvation levels.

The film takes place in 1933, the depths of the Great Depression. Note how the Joads and other families lose their land and homes. Also note the conditions that await them in California in the labor camps.

(continued)

It is important for you to know that this film has been the continuing subject of controversy. Many critics felt that the harsh indictments in Steinbeck's novel were softened in the film. They argued that the director focused too much on one family, the Joads, and their struggle to keep together as a unit, rather than on the more universal theme of the economic and political inequities of this time period. Other critics felt that this film had too much of a "message" and not enough entertainment value. What do you think about the purpose of films in general and whether their only function is to entertain?

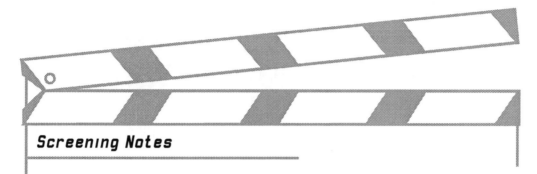

Screening Notes

THE GRAPES OF WRATH

VOCABULARY

dust bowl   sharecropper

Okies   homicide

migrant worker

QUESTIONS BASED ON THE FILM

1. According to Muley, what makes his land belong to him?

   _____

   _____

   _____

2. Contrast the superintendent or land agent with the sharecroppers as he comes to tell them to leave the land.

   _____

   _____

   _____

3. How are the Joads helped at the roadside diner in New Mexico?

   _____

   _____

   _____

(continued)

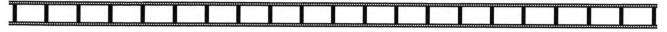

4. What is the reaction of the service station attendants to the Okies before they set out across the desert?

_____

_____

_____

5. Why are the Okies met with hostility and suspicion by the native Californians?

_____

_____

_____

_____

6. Contrast the camp at the Keene Ranch with the Farmworker's Wheat Patch Camp.

_____

_____

_____

_____

TEACHER'S GUIDE

AIR FORCE

Warner Brothers, 1943; directed by Howard Hawks, black and white, 124 minutes

BACKGROUND OF THE FILM

Starting with the historical fact that a squadron of B-17s arrived in Hawaii during the Japanese attack on Pearl Harbor, *Air Force* traces the adventures of one fictional bomber crew across the Pacific to the Philippines, to the Battle of the Coral Sea, to a crash landing on an Australian beach. The movie received help from the Army Air Corps because General Hap Arnold saw the need for a movie that would show the American people the Air Force in action. In writing the script, Dudley Nichols had at his disposal battle reports supplied by the War Department and the technical advice of Captain Samuel Triffy, an Air Corps pilot. The plot, which grew out of the collaboration of Nichols, Triffy, and director Howard Hawks, proved to be little more than a vehicle for portraying the Air Force winning the war almost single-handedly.

Air Force in fact anticipated history—sometimes by months, sometimes by years. The climactic air-sea battle, created with miniatures and special effects, might have borne a vague resemblance to the battles of the Coral Sea and Midway. Yet, it had been staged and filmed before the actual battles had taken place. B-17s did participate in both actions, although not in the manner portrayed in the film.

Despite its mythical-cum-historical narrative, *Air Force* did more than entertain the American people. The movie slaughter of the Japanese fleet provided a catharsis for the setbacks suffered at Pearl Harbor,

Wake Island, and the Philippines. Tied into the plot were continuous overt and subtle propaganda messages, conveyed in terms that were becoming familiar to wartime moviegoers. The crew of the *Mary Ann* consisted of a heterogeneous cross section of the nation except for an African American. The crew is diverse and fractious, but against all others its members unite and take care of each other, and everyone does his assigned job for the good of the plane.

In contrast, the Japanese are all characterized as sneaky and treacherous and throughout the film are referred to in derogatory terms. This message is constantly reinforced, beginning with the opening scenes. On the way to Hawaii, the crew hears a news broadcast that a Japanese peace envoy was planning to meet with Secretary of State Hull on the morning of December 7. When the plane lands at Pearl Harbor, the crew is immediately told of Japanese sabotage of American planes before the attack (historically untrue). The Japanese are portrayed as fighting unfairly, attacking without warning, and shooting at a helpless flier as he parachutes from his disabled plane. Not only are the Japanese shown as evil, but they are also shown as inferior in fair combat. The *Mary Ann* shoots down Japanese plane after plane, and the Air Force sinks the entire enemy fleet.

The message stands out clearly: The United States will win the war; we may have lost the first round through deceit, but victory will be ours. The movie's prophecy of victory, repeated enough times, would inevitably have a positive influence on the war effort.

SYNOPSIS OF THE PLOT

On the evening of December 6, 1941, the *Mary Ann*, a B-17 bomber, takes off on a training mission to Hawaii. As the plane travels across the Pacific, the ethnic and geographic diversity of the crew is emphasized, as is the estrangement of one of its members (Sergeant Winocki) from the service. The crew of the plane learns of the Japanese attack on Pearl Harbor and the *Mary Ann* is diverted to a small emergency landing field. The plane is attacked by fifth columnists; the *Mary Ann* takes off and lands at Hickam Field, where the evidence of the Japanese attack is still very apparent.

The crew next receives orders to fly to the Philippines by way of Wake Island. They are joined by Lieutenant Tex Rader, a fighter pilot who is being assigned to Manila. The friendly rivalry between bomber and fighter crews is shown in the conversation en route. The *Mary Ann* arrives at Wake Island, where a small number of U.S. Marines are preparing for a defense against a much larger Japanese force. The only passenger the plane picks up at Wake Island is a dog named Tripoli, who goes into a rage at the mention of Tojo's name.

When the bomber arrives in the Philippines, they hear accounts of how the Americans are outnumbered but still are superior fighters to the Japanese. The crew chief, White, learns that his son has been killed. The *Mary Ann* takes off to avoid a Japanese air strike and goes in search of the invasion fleet. Instead, the B-17 runs into a squadron of Japanese planes and, in a display of American superiority, shoots down plane after plane. Vastly outnumbered, the bomber receives numerous hits and the pilot, Quincannon, is mortally wounded. The crew bails out except for Winocki, who belly-lands the plane at Clark Field.

The crew arrives back at the base to be by Quincannon's bedside when he dies. They promise to repair the *Mary Ann* and have the plane fly once more. In a race to become airborne before the Japanese arrive, the crew works on the bomber. Private Chester volunteers to fly as a tail gunner on an observation plane. When his plane is hit by a Japanese zero, he

parachutes and is machine-gunned to death in a dramatic display of Japanese treachery and barbarism. At the very last minute, while the enemy reaches the airfield, the *Mary Ann,* now piloted by Rader, takes off and heads towards Australia.

When the *Mary Ann* comes upon the Japanese fleet, the bomber radios the information to Allied air bases and ships. When a huge formation of American planes arrives, the *Mary Ann* leads them in the attack, slaughtering the Japanese fleet. Short of fuel, the *Mary Ann* is forced to crash-land in the surf on a beach in Australia. The closing scene shows the surviving crew members preparing to attack Tokyo with a squadron of bombers, an event that historically did not begin until 1944.

IDEAS FOR CLASS DISCUSSION

This film lends itself to a discussion of propaganda. What is and isn't propaganda? Is this film a piece of propaganda? What elements of it can be identified as propagandistic? Is propaganda ever justified? The crew of the *Mary Ann* represents the archetypical American melting pot of the World War II era. Almost every World War II combat film that dwelt on a small combat unit mirrored that composition. Its composition, and the particular groups missing from it, make an excellent discussion topic. It also might prove productive to discuss the internment of the Japanese during World War II and the attitudes that are portrayed in *Air Force.*

BOOKS AND MATERIALS RELATING TO THIS FILM AND TOPIC

Blum, John Morton. *V Was for Victory: Politics and American Culture During World War II.* New York: Harcourt Brace Jovanovich, 1976.

Dower, John W. *War Without Mercy: Race and Power in the Pacific War.* New York: Pantheon, 1987.

Fussell, Paul. *Wartime: Understanding and Behavior in the Second World War.* New York: Oxford University Press, 1989.

Koppes, Clayton R., and Gregory D. Black. *Hollywood Goes to War: How Politics, Profits, and Propaganda Shaped World War II Movies.* New York: The Free Press, 1987.

Orriss, Bruce W. *When Hollywood Ruled the Skies.* Hawthorne, CA: Aero Associates, 1984.

Schaffer, Ronald. *Wings of Judgment: American Bombing in World War II.* New York: Oxford University Press, 1985.

Suid, Lawrence Howard, ed. *Air Force.* Madison, WI: University of Wisconsin Press, 1983.

———*Guts and Glory: Great American War Movies.* Reading, MA: Addison Wesley, 1978.

Terkel, Studs. *The Good War: An Oral History of World War II.* New York: Pantheon, 1984.

OTHER MEDIA RESOURCES FOR THIS TIME PERIOD

The Battle of the Bulge (1965, 141 minutes) A workmanlike telling of the stopping of the last desperate German offensive; the video has been cut by 23 minutes, making the story less intelligible than it was originally.

Band of Brothers (2002, 10 hours) Emmy Award-winning miniseries about a World War II army rifle company that parachuted into France on D-day

A Bridge Too Far (1977, 175 minutes) Sir Richard Attenborough's careful (some say at the expense of dramatic impact) reconstruction of Operation Market Garden; it is based on Cornelius Ryan's last book.

Come See the Paradise (1990, 138 minutes) Romance that revolves around the internment of Japanese-Americans during the war; rated **R**

Fat Man and Little Boy (1989, 126 minutes) The somewhat fictionalized story of the Manhattan Project—the building of the atomic bomb—with Paul Newman as General Leslie Groves, the military engineer and builder of the Pentagon who was given the job of producing a nuclear weapon before the Germans did

Go For Broke! (1951, 92 minutes) Story of Japanese-American soldiers who fought in Europe and distinguished themselves during World War II

Ike: The War Years (1978, 196 minutes) The edited version of a six-hour television miniseries starring Robert Duvall; its central events are the D-day invasion and Ike's "romance" with his driver Kay Summersby (played by Lee Remick).

The Longest Day (1962, 180 minutes) Darryl Zanuck's epic all-star recreation of the D-day invasion; it was the first of these docudramas and some think the best.

MacArthur (1977, 130 minutes) Gregory Peck plays the controversial general, from his assumption of military command in the Pacific to his firing by President Truman, in a film that takes a middle course between genius and megalomania in assessing his character.

Memphis Belle (1990, 106 minutes) The composite and partly fictional story of a single B-17 crew as it prepares for and carries out its last mission over Europe; it is based on William Wyler's wartime composite documentary of the same title, which is also available on film and video (42 minutes).

Midway (1976, 135 minutes) The epic "all-star" reconstruction of the carrier battle that ended the Japanese expansion in the Pacific; the version available on video leaves out the Battle of the Coral Sea section that provides essential background to the Midway decisions and leaves in the fictional (and silly) Charlton Heston love story.

Patton (1970, 171 minutes) Features George C. Scott's riveting and troubling portrayal of the general, from North Africa to his death

Pearl Harbor (2001, 183 minutes) More a soap opera than a historical depiction of this event; the special effects won an Academy Award®.

PT 109 (1963, 140 minutes) The story of John F. Kennedy's service during World War II, based on Kennedy's own account; Cliff Robertson was chosen with the approval of the president to play him. Since Kennedy's death, questions about this episode have arisen among historians, but none of this is reflected in the film.

Saving Private Ryan (1998, 169 minutes) Three brothers are killed during World War II, and the U.S. government sets out to find the fourth brother who is somewhere behind enemy lines. Rated **R**

They Were Expendable (1945, 136 minutes) John Ford's personal version of the PT squadrons that harried the Japanese invasion of the Philippines in early 1942; it starred Robert Montgomery and John Wayne.

Thin Red Line (1998, 170 minutes) Focuses on the Battle of Guadalcanal and the soldiers who form a tight-knit group in the appalling conditions of battle. Rated **R**

To Hell and Back (1955, 196 minutes) The sanitized autobiographical film about (and starring) Audie Murphy, who was America's most decorated soldier in World War II, receiving 24 medals for valor, including the Congressional Medal of Honor

Tora, Tora, Tora (1970, 161 minutes) An American-Japanese coproduction about the bombing of Pearl Harbor

Tuskegee Airmen (1995, 106 minutes) Film about the first African-American pilots allowed to fight in World War II

Twelve O'Clock High (1949, 132 minutes) The story of the war toll as a result of ordering young men to their deaths in the first high-risk days of the American daylight bombing campaign over Europe; Gregory Peck plays General Frank Savage and Dean Jagger his adjutant, Major Harvey Stoval. Jagger won an Oscar® for his performance.

Windtalkers (2002, 133 minutes) During World War II, Navajoes were used as communication specialists because the Japanese could not decipher their language. Rated **R**

In addition to these, there are documentaries on specific aspects of the war as it affected American life. The best of these include *The Homefront* (1985, 90 minutes), available in three parts with a companion book; *The Life and Times of Rosie the Riveter* (1980, 65 minutes); *Silver Wings and Santiago Blue* (1984, 88 minutes), about women pilots during World War II; *A Question of Loyalty* (1982, 50 minutes) and *Nisei Soldier* (1984, 30 minutes), both about the wartime internment on the U.S. West Coast of Americans of Japanese ancestry.

——— AIR FORCE ———

Warner Brothers, 1943; directed by Howard Hawks

Major Character	Actor/Actress
Captain Mike Quincannon	John Ridgely
Lieutenant Bill Williams	Gig Young
Lieutenant Tommy McMartin	Arthur Kennedy
Lieutenant Monk Hauser	Charles Drake
Sergeant Robby White	Harry Carey
Corporal Weinberg	George Tobias
Corporal Peterson	Ward Wood
Private Chester	Ray Montgomery
Sergeant Joe Winocki	John Garfield
Lieutenant Tex Rader	James Brown

WHAT TO WATCH FOR

Air Force was a major box-office success and a great morale builder for Americans during World War II. After the Japanese attack on Pearl Harbor and their rapid conquest of the Pacific, Americans needed to hear and see a message of hope; *Air Force* provided this.

Watch for examples of propaganda throughout the entire film, such as the constantly repeated theme that America will eventually win the war. Through treachery and deceit on the part of the Japanese, America has lost the first round, but in a fair fight, we will persevere and victory will ultimately be ours.

The movie is a blend of truth and fiction. Japanese fifth columnists (enemy sympathizers who sabotage within a country) *did not* damage any planes in Hawaii. The air-sea battle was created with miniatures and filmed *before* the battles of the

(continued)

Coral Sea and Midway had taken place. Regular bombing raids of Japan *did not* begin until 1944 and were carried out by B-29 Super Fortresses, not the B-17s as portrayed in the film.

Note how the Japanese are all characterized as sneaky and treacherous and throughout the film are referred to in derogatory terms. They have been successful because they do not fight fairly, but the film shows the Americans are superior in combat. Remember when this film was produced and what was happening in the world. This film was produced with the help of the Army Air Corps to bolster morale and contribute to the war effort.

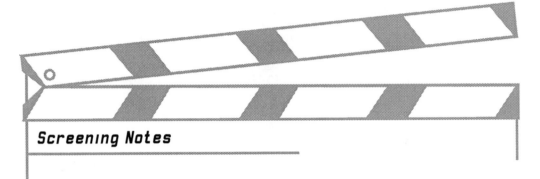

Screening Notes

—— **AIR FORCE** ——

VOCABULARY

B-17 bomber   fifth column
Pearl Harbor   sabotage
bombardier   Mr. Moto
"Rising Sun"

QUESTIONS BASED ON THE FILM

1. What characteristics do Americans display in the film? How do these characteristics combine to ensure an American victory in a fair fight?

   _____

   _____

   _____

2. According to the film, why is the attack on Pearl Harbor particularly treacherous?

   _____

   _____

3. Give three examples from the film that were meant to portray the Japanese as deceitful and winning by unfair fighting.

   _____

   _____

   _____

(continued)

4. Why do the marines give their dog to the crew of the *Mary Ann*?

_____

_____

_____

5. In a paragraph, explain how this film might have raised American morale during World War II.

_____

_____

_____

_____

_____

_____

UNIT 11

The Cold War

TEACHER'S GUIDE

DR. STRANGELOVE OR: HOW I LEARNED TO STOP WORRYING AND LOVE THE BOMB

Columbia Pictures, 1964; written, produced, and directed by Stanley Kubrick, black and white, 93 minutes

BACKGROUND OF THE FILM

Hollywood had almost always portrayed the U.S. military as infallible and heroic (see, for example, *Air Force*). This changed in the early 1960s, particularly after the nuclear war scare and peaceful solution of the Cuban missile crisis, when the Cold War appeared to be thawing. Also, new producers and directors had appeared during the 1950s who were socially conscious and not dependent upon the military for any assistance, and thus able to make antiestablishment movies. The atomic bomb and its use as a nuclear threat became a topic for several movies that portrayed the military and nuclear brinkmanship in a very critical light. Stanley Kubrick's film is one of these. Kubrick had previously directed the antiwar film *Paths of Glory* (1958), about French Army mutinies during World War I, and *Spartacus* (1960) about the Roman slave revolt. *Dr. Strangelove,* which he wrote, produced, and directed, is one of the best-known of these movies. He would go on to write, produce, and direct *2001: A Space Odyssey* in 1969, *A Clockwork Orange* in 1971, and *Full Metal Jacket* in 1987.

Dr. Strangelove was suggested to Kubrick by the novel *Red Alert* by Peter George, a thriller about an accidental nuclear attack. Originally, Kubrick's movie was to be a serious suspense film, but he found satire

and black comedy were the best ways to tell the story and make his point.

Since the military often provided technical assistance and material resources to film producers making war movies, Kubrick actually approached the U.S. Air Force to discuss the film. In this instance, the Air Force refused to provide any cooperation, based not only on the film's proposed portrayal of its officers as deranged and ludicrous, but on what the Pentagon regarded as a misrepresentation of the Positive Control safeguards against an accidental or unauthorized nuclear attack. According to the Air Force, General Ripper's one-man decision to launch a nuclear assault on the Soviet Union would be impossible because an SAC (Strategic Air Command) officer cannot order such an attack. Only the president has the attack code, which is relayed to SAC headquarters. According to the military, this system was "fail-safe"; it could not be subverted. Kubrick did much research on the subject and disagreed that it was fail-safe.

Several historians believe that *Dr. Strangelove* strikes at some commonly held attitudes of the Cold War era: American anti-Communist paranoia, blind faith in modern technology, and the lack of a true understanding of the enormity of a nuclear war. (See for example Charles Maland's article "Dr. Strangelove: Nightmare Comedy and the Ideology of Liberal Consensus," in Peter C. Rollins's *Hollywood as Historian,* University of Kentucky Press, 1983.) The character of Ripper satirizes the Cold War paranoia towards communism that even regarded the fluoridation of water as a Communist conspiracy. Dr.

Strangelove appears as a bizarre composite of nuclear theorists. Many filmgoers identified him as a composite of army missile project director Wernher von Braun and nuclear war theorists Herman Kahn and Henry Kissinger. Major King Kong's speech to his crew is more like a traditional World War II pep talk than a speech appropriate for someone about to participate in the destruction of the world. Note also the survival kit each crewman receives and the irony of worrying about such things in the event of a nuclear war.

This is a complex movie in many ways, with numerous examples of satire and possible innuendos. Is, for example, President Muffley supposed to be reminiscent of Democratic liberal Adlai Stevenson? There have been numerous articles written about the film, particularly in the 1980s. When it was released, *Dr. Strangelove* received mixed reviews ranging from those attacking it as a disservice to the nation to those praising it as the best American film in years. An interesting side note is that when SAC commander General Curtis LeMay found out about *Dr. Strangelove,* he encouraged the making of the Rock Hudson film *A Gathering of Eagles* to show that Air Force officers were competent and that fail-safe safeguards did exist to prevent an accidental or unauthorized attack like that portrayed in Kubrick's film. It is also interesting to note that there were three other "doomsday" films produced at around the same time: *Fail Safe* (1964), based on the Eugene Burdick and Harvey Wheeler novel; *Seven Days in May* (1964), from a Rod Serling script about a military coup to prevent peace being made with Russia; and *The Bedford Incident* (1965), based on a novel by Mark Rascovich, about an unintended nuclear exchange at sea.

SYNOPSIS OF THE PLOT

The action opens at Turpleson Air Force Base when British liaison officer Group Captain Mandrake receives a phone call from Air Force General Ripper that he is putting the base on Condition Red. The scene then cuts to a B-52 bomber, where a top-secret coded message comes through ordering the aircraft to attack Russia. The pilot, Major Kong, can't believe the message and asks for a confirmation of the order.

At General Turgidson's "love nest" in Washington, a phone call comes through and he is told that an attack plan has been put into effect and that General Ripper has sealed off the base. On board Major Kong's plane, the crew members prepare for the attack and open their secret orders. At the base, Mandrake questions Ripper's orders.

At the Pentagon in the War Room, the president is meeting with Turgidson and other commanders. Turgidson tries to explain what has happened and excitedly points out its possibilities. Instead, the Russian Ambassador de Sadesky, wearing a hidden camera, is brought into the War Room and the president contacts Premier Kissov on the hot line. The president tells the premier about the attack and advises him to shoot the American bombers down since they cannot be recalled. The premier tells the ambassador about the existence of a "doomsday machine," which is programmed to automatically respond to any aggression by detonating nuclear weapons that will make the earth uninhabitable for 99 years. The ambassador relays this to the president and officers.

Back at the base, an army unit, led by Colonel Guano, is trying to break through base security forces. Ripper tells Mandrake that the Communists are involved in a plot to poison the world by fluoridation. When the Air Force security troops surrender, Mandrake tries to coax Ripper into telling him the recall code. Ripper shoots himself.

The planes are rapidly approaching their targets. Kong's plane is hit by a missile, but the pilot is able to continue on despite the damage.

At the base, Mandrake is confronted by Colonel Guano. Mandrake tries to convince him that he knows the recall code and must call the president. Eventually, Mandrake gets through via a pay phone (finding change for the phone causes a confrontation between Mandrake and Guano). All of the planes are recalled except for Kong's plane, which does not receive the message since its radio is damaged. As the plane approaches the target, it is discovered that the bomb doors won't open. Kong climbs onto the bomb, gets the doors to open, and rides the bomb to its target.

Back in the War Room, Dr. Strangelove recommends that everyone move to a deep mine shaft for 100 years to survive the radioactivity released by the doomsday machine. With growing excitement, he speaks of a new master race and, as if by uncontrollable reflex, reverts to his Nazi roots. The movie ends as mushroom clouds appear and the song "We'll Meet Again Someday" plays.

IDEAS FOR CLASS DISCUSSION

With the end of the Cold War and the gradual "builddown" of nuclear weapons, a film like *Dr. Strangelove* may seem a bit old-fashioned to students. But the issue of who controls the button that might unleash global destruction is still vital—perhaps more complex now than it was in the bipolar world of the early 1960s. Chernobyl and Three Mile Island remind us that it is not only in weapons that nuclear technology poses a potential threat. Many more nations have joined, or are reputed to have joined, the "nuclear club," but global annihilation can now be accomplished chemically and biologically as well. Scares involving anthrax and smallpox serve to illustrate that nuclear disaster is not the only threat to civilization as we know it. Discussion that updates the concerns and fears expressed in *Dr. Strangelove* would be very interesting. In addition, discussion can focus on the aspects of the Cold War (ideas, technologies, prejudices, personalities, events) that the film reflects and satirizes.

BOOKS AND MATERIALS RELATING TO THIS FILM AND TOPIC

George, Peter. *Red Alert*. Ace, 1958.

Kagan, Norman. *The Cinema of Stanley Kubrick*. New York: Grove Press, 1972.

Kahn, Herman. *On Thermonuclear War*. Princeton, NJ: Princeton University Press, 1961.

Kissinger, Henry. *Nuclear Weapons and Foreign Policy*. New York: Harper, 1957.

Whitfield, Stephen J. *The Culture of the Cold War*. Baltimore: Johns Hopkins, 1990.

Wittner, Lawrence S. *Cold War America: From Hiroshima to Watergate*. New York: Praeger, 1974.

OTHER MEDIA RESOURCES FOR THIS TIME PERIOD

Eleanor, First Lady of the World (1982, 98 minutes) Film about Eleanor Roosevelt's activist role after World War II and the death of her husband

The Front (1976, 95 minutes) Woody Allen movie about a restaurant worker who helps blacklisted writers by submitting scripts under his name

Guilty by Suspicion (1991, 105 minutes) A Hollywood director is blacklisted by the House Committee on Un-American Activities and is unable to find work.

The Manchurian Candidate (1962, 126 minutes) This story about brainwashing, power, and political assassination was withdrawn from circulation by its star, Frank Sinatra, when John F. Kennedy was killed.

Missiles of October (1974, 155 minutes) Made-for-television movie based upon RFK's book about the Cuban missile crisis of 1962

On the Beach (1959, 133 minutes) One of the first films to warn of the threat of nuclear holocaust

The Russians Are Coming! The Russians Are Coming! (1966, 120 minutes) One of the first films to break down the stereotype of the Russians as our mortal enemies

Thirteen Days (2000, 145 minutes) Set during the two-week time period of the Cuban missile crisis of 1962

WarGames (1983, 114 minutes) Raises the safety issues surrounding computer command and control of nuclear weapons

DR. STRANGELOVE OR: HOW I LEARNED TO STOP WORRYING AND LOVE THE BOMB

Columbia Pictures, 1964; written, produced, and directed by Stanley Kubrick

Major Character	Actor/Actress
General Jack D. Ripper	Sterling Hayden
General Buck Turgidson	George C. Scott
President Merkin Muffley	Peter Sellers
Group Captain Lionel Mandrake	Peter Sellers
Dr. Strangelove	Peter Sellers
Major "King" Kong	Slim Pickens
Ambassador de Sadesky	Peter Bull
Colonel Bat Guano	Keenan Wynn

WHAT TO WATCH FOR

This controversial film was one of the first in the Cold War era to show the military in a critical light and to point out the reality of a possible nuclear incident. The Strategic Air Command (SAC) declared its nuclear weapons launch-control system to be "fail-safe"—that is, incapable of being activated by either human insubordination or machine error. In spite of this, Stanley Kubrick, the director of *Dr. Strangelove,* felt otherwise. He wished to illustrate the seriousness of the nuclear threat as well as the paranoia shown by many Americans towards communism.

Kubrick used satire and black comedy to drive home his concerns. *Black comedy* is comedy that straddles a fine line between horror and humor. It portrays things of such a serious nature that laughter is the only way to break the tension. Some critics wrote that the film was so ludicrous in some ways and in other instances so humorous that it missed its primary objective.

(continued)

Keep in mind the time in which this film was produced. The Cuban missile crisis (October 1962) was a recent memory. Despite the signing of the Nuclear Test Ban Treaty in 1963, the United States military was calling for more missiles, bombers, and bombs to defend against the Soviet Union. The thaw in the Cold War had not yet reached the military establishment. Also, strategic planners in both countries were putting into place a deterrence theory based upon targeting nuclear weapons at one another's cities. If either side started a war, both sides would suffer mutually assured destruction. The resulting theory, which governed both sides' nuclear policy, was called M.A.D.D. for "Mutually Assured Destruction Doctrine." Kubrick's film was a response to this.

The film also proved a great vehicle for one of the most versatile comic actors of the day, Peter Sellers. Much of our current comedy, particularly in programs like *Saturday Night Live,* owes much to the genius of Sellers.

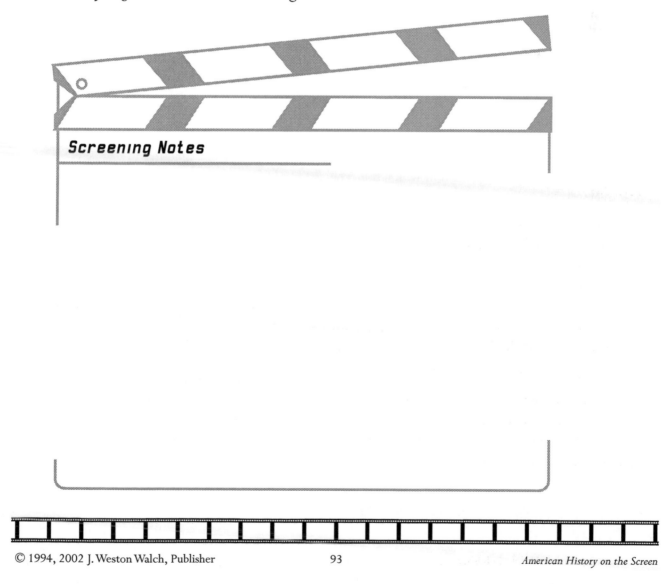

Screening Notes

DR. STRANGELOVE OR: HOW I LEARNED TO STOP WORRYING AND LOVE THE BOMB

VOCABULARY

fail-safe

ICBM (intercontinental ballistic missile)

megaton

Pentagon

M.A.D.D.

safeguard

Strategic Air Command

guano

turgid

King Kong

Jack the Ripper

QUESTIONS BASED ON THE FILM

1. Does Major Kong's pep talk to his crew, with its accompanying background music, seem appropriate to the situation in which the crew finds itself? What message is Kubrick trying to present in this scene?

   _____

   _____

   _____

2. What does General Ripper do to secure his base?

   _____

   _____

   _____

(continued)

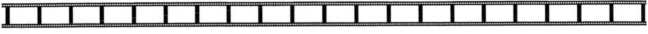

3. Why can't the planes be immediately recalled?

_____

_____

_____

4. What is General Turgidson's answer to the "problem" of the attack without presidential authorization?

_____

_____

_____

5. According to de Sadesky, why did the Russians build the doomsday machine?

_____

_____

_____

6. What are the characteristics of "real Americans" as General Turgidson, General Ripper, Colonel Guano, and Major Kong might each define them?

_____

_____

_____

_____

7. According to Ripper, what massive Communist conspiracy began in 1946?

_____

_____

_____

(continued)

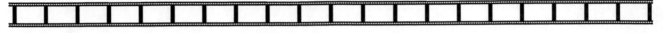

8. According to Dr. Strangelove, how should the president determine who should survive in the mine shafts? What long-term benefits to the United States might result from the impending nuclear holocaust?

    _____

    _____

    _____

    _____

9. Was there some reason beyond a director's desire to get "maximum mileage" from his comedy star that Stanley Kubrick had Peter Sellers play the three particular characters (Group Captain Mandrake, President Muffley, and Dr. Strangelove) that he does in the film?

    _____

    _____

    _____

    _____

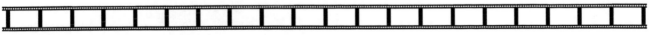

The Civil Rights Movement

TEACHER'S GUIDE

THE LONG WALK HOME

New Visions Pictures, 1991; directed by Richard Pearce, color, 97 minutes

BACKGROUND OF THE FILM

On December 1, 1955, Rosa Parks was riding home from her job as a seamstress in a downtown Montgomery, Alabama, department store. When the bus driver ordered her to give up her seat to a white passenger as the law required, Mrs. Parks refused. She was arrested and put in jail. The next morning a group of black community leaders including Ralph Abernathy, pastor of the First Baptist Church, called for a one-day boycott of the Montgomery city buses on the day of Rosa Parks's trial. The pastor of the Dexter Avenue Baptist Church, Martin Luther King, Jr., made his church available for meetings. The boycott was supported by such a large proportion of the African-American riding public that it was extended.

This film is about two Montgomery families and their experiences during the boycott. The Thompsons are white and affluent; Miriam Thompson is wrapped up in her social round of Junior League bridge parties and hairdresser's appointments. Odessa Cotter is the Thompsons' maid who must walk nine miles from her home with its meager simplicity to the Thompsons' suburban residence.

When this film was released in 1990, it was almost immediately withdrawn because a critic, who said he was in Montgomery during the boycott, questioned the film's premise. It was later discovered that this critic had not been in Montgomery, and the film was rereleased in 1991 with the endorsement of Rosa Parks and many African-American leaders.

The film gives a good view of racial attitudes in the segregated South of the 1950s, as well as an interesting glimpse at Miriam Thompson's increasing self-awareness. The Montgomery bus boycott is viewed by many as one of the primary moving events of the Civil Rights movement, a shining example of the nonviolent protest that culminated 55 weeks later in the city ending the legal segregation of public transportation.

SYNOPSIS OF THE PLOT

The movie takes place in 1955 in Montgomery, Alabama. The opening scene shows African-American women entering a bus through the front door, paying their fare, then getting off and entering the bus again through the back door. The story is told from seven-year-old Mary Catherine Thompson's point of view. Odessa Cotter is the Thompson family's maid.

Odessa is told by Miriam Thompson to take Mary Catherine and some friends to the park for a picnic. A policeman throws Odessa out of the whites-only park. Miriam uses her political pull with the police commissioner to force the policeman to apologize to Odessa.

At Odessa's house, her two boys bring notice of a boycott of the buses. Rosa Parks has been arrested for sitting down and refusing to give up her seat to a white person. The next morning the buses go by empty. Miriam decides to pick Odessa up when she calls to say she'll be late to work because she will not ride the bus.

In the evenings, there are meetings to unify and inspire the people as the bus boycott continues. Odessa and her family attend these meetings.

Miriam becomes concerned that Odessa's long walk to and from work is wearing her out. She agrees to pick Odessa up two mornings a week. The police follow Miriam in an effort to harass her. Miriam's husband, Norman, doesn't know that Miriam is bringing Odessa to work. When Miriam questions his involvement in a citizen's group to fight the boycott, Norm is furious. When Norm finds out that Miriam is driving Odessa, he forbids her to do it again.

Miriam confronts Norman and tells him not to meddle in the way she runs the household. His reaction is to withdraw to another part of the house and question their entire relationship. Miriam now decides to support the bus boycott actively by volunteering to drive a carpool from the city to the suburbs.

Norm's brother, Tunker, takes Norm to the carpool rendezvous where a group of white businessmen have assembled to harass the people waiting for rides. Tunker threatens Miriam, but when he slaps her, Norman goes to her rescue.

Despite the threats and shouts of the white men, the black women stand firm. As they join hands and sing a spiritual, Miriam joins them.

IDEAS FOR CLASS DISCUSSION

Enough time has now passed since the era of the early Civil Rights movement for us to begin to analyze and examine it in films such as *Malcolm X* and *Eyes on the Prize*. A fruitful class discussion might be to look at how far we have come, what inequalities still need to be addressed, and what methods might properly be used to address these issues effectively. This could be extended to a discussion of gender issues, cultural bias, and the question of sexual orientation.

BOOKS AND MATERIALS RELATING TO THIS FILM AND TOPIC

Cooney, Robert, and Helen Michalowski, eds. *The Power of the People: Active Nonviolence in the United States*. Philadelphia: New Society Publishers, 1987.

King, Martin Luther, Jr. *Stride Toward Freedom: The Montgomery Story*. New York: Harper and Row, 1958.

OTHER MEDIA RESOURCES FOR THIS TIME PERIOD

Ali (2001, 156 minutes) Biography of legendary boxer Muhammad Ali; rated **R**

The Court Martial of Jackie Robinson (1990, 93 minutes) Directed by Larry Pearce; after experiencing racism on his army base, Robinson refuses to give up his seat in the front of an army bus and is court-martialed for insubordination.

Crisis at Central High (1981, 120 minutes) A made-for-television movie starring Joanne Woodward about the federally mandated desegregation of the Little Rock, Arkansas, public schools

Driving Miss Daisy (1989, 99 minutes) Academy Award®-winning film about the relationship between an elderly white woman and her African-American chauffer

King (1978, 272 minute) Directed by Abby Mann; the made-for-television dramatization of the life of civil rights leader Martin Luther King, Jr.

Malcolm X (1992, 201 minutes) Directed by Spike Lee; the superb, if occasionally romanticized, account of the spiritual journey of the black Muslim leader from his troubled childhood until his assassination

Ruby Bridges (1998, 90 minutes) A Disney movie about a six-year-old girl who participated in the integration of schools in New Orleans in 1960

THE LONG WALK HOME

New Visions Pictures, 1991; directed by Richard Pearce

Major Character	Actor/Actress
Odessa Cotter	Whoopi Goldberg
Miriam Thompson	Sissy Spacek
Norman Thompson	Dwight Schultz
Tunker Thompson	Dylan Baker
Cotter	Ving Rhames

WHAT TO WATCH FOR

The Montgomery bus boycott of 1955–56 was in a very real sense the beginning of the Civil Rights movement in the American South. This film portrays the events of the boycott through the eyes of two families: the affluent white family, the Thompsons, and the family of their African-American maid, Odessa Cotter. The screenwriter of the film, John Cork, grew up in Montgomery, so the behaviors and look of the film are accurate.

Although it may seem shocking today, the attitudes expressed by the whites in the film were not atypical of that time period. It is important to note that, despite the existence of the racist white citizen's group, which Norm Thompson joins in the film, there were many whites in Montgomery who did support the boycott. The well-organized carpool system portrayed did, in fact, exist.

The minister of the church where the African Americans go for support is the Reverend Martin Luther King, Jr. The Montgomery bus boycott was King's first real success with nonviolent protest.

(continued)

Note the increasing tension between Miriam and her husband. This film also deals with Miriam's growing independence and individualism.

This film was endorsed by Rosa Parks, the woman who "began it all" when on December 1, 1955, she refused to give her bus seat to a white person, which was the law at that time.*

* Not only was public transportation in the South segregated; drinking fountains, restaurants, restrooms, and movie-theater entrances were labeled "whites only" or "colored." The Civil Rights movement sought to change these restrictive and discriminatory laws.

Screening Notes

—— *THE LONG WALK HOME* —————————————

VOCABULARY

boycott   segregation
the Klan

QUESTIONS BASED ON THE FILM

1. Why are the African-American residents of Montgomery boycotting the city buses?

    _____

    _____

    _____

2. Compare Christmas at the Thompson household with that at the Cotters.

    _____

    _____

    _____

3. What are some of the attitudes expressed by the Thompson relatives about Negroes?

    _____

    _____

    _____

(continued)

4. What happens to Selma when she tries to ride the bus to the other side of town?

_____

_____

_____

_____

5. How does Miriam change during the course of the film?

_____

_____

_____

_____

6. What is the reaction of the African-American citizens when they hear that Dr. King's house has been bombed?

_____

_____

_____

_____

7. Is the boycott successful? Why is this event so significant in the civil rights?

_____

_____

_____

_____

TEACHER'S GUIDE

AMERICAN GRAFFITI

Universal Pictures, 1972; directed by George
Lucas, color, 110 minutes

BACKGROUND OF THE FILM

George Lucas was only 28 years old when he
conceived the idea for *American Graffiti* and went on
to direct the movie. Students will know Lucas better
for the *Star Wars* series and the *Indiana Jones* movies,
but this was his first big hit.

American Graffiti, the first big 1950s nostalgia
movie, captures the last moments of American "innocence" before the turbulent 1960s took hold. The
time is 1962 and the setting is Modesto, California.
Lucas graduated from a high school in Modesto in
1962, and the movie is drawn from his experiences as
a teenager. To teenagers in Modesto, cruising—that
is, riding up and down the main street showing off
your car to other teenagers—was a way of life. Lucas
himself cruised the streets every day from three in the
afternoon until 1:00 A.M. The hub of activity was the
drive-in restaurant— Mel's Drive-in in the movie.
Lucas based his main characters on people he knew in
high school: Steve is the all-American boy, class president, and athlete; Milner is a greaser with cigarettes
in his rolled-up T-shirt sleeve; Toad is the classic nerd
and loser; Curt is the class brain, always quick with a
retort; Laurie is head cheerleader, a "good" girl who
refuses to have sex with Steve before he goes off to
college; Debbie is the "bad" girl who is willing to "put
out" for liquor and a nice car.

The actors and actresses playing the roles in *American Graffiti* were relative unknowns when the film was
made. Now, of course, they are instantly recognized;

many went on to become major Hollywood stars.
Ron Howard was already a television child star; he
is now even better known as a director of hit films,
including *Apollo 13* and *A Beautiful Mind.*

The film was budgeted at $700,000, a very low
sum even in 1972. It took only 28 nights to shoot.
All of the action is compressed into one late summer
night and revolves around the parallel adventures and
misadventures of the four male friends: Steve Bolan-
der, Curt Henderson, Terry "Toad" Fields, and John
Milner. Adults in the film rarely appear; when they do
they are pictured as fools, like the high school principal who gives Steve detention, only to be reminded
that he has already graduated, or the policemen
whose car is separated from its wheels in the prank
played by the Pharaohs gang. The only significant adult
in this world populated by teenagers is Wolfman Jack,
a real-life legendary figure from the late 1950s. He
became famous as a disc jockey on a Mexican radio
station that could be heard from coast to coast. The
Wolfman becomes a Wizard of Oz-like character, part
of the teen's world of fantasy. But in reality, as Curt
finds out, he is really a great pretender. Wolfman and
his music are a connecting thread throughout the film.

American Graffiti went on to make Universal
Studios a profit of $350 million. It started a nostalgia
craze that resulted in television shows like *Happy Days*
and *Laverne and Shirley.* Baby boomers, disillusioned by
the strife-torn America of the 1960s, nostalgically
relived their 1950s youth as a time when there was
a sense of community in shared values, language,
humor, and music. As Dale Pollock, author of
Skywalking: The Life and Films of George Lucas, writes:

103

"The secret of the success of *Graffiti* is that it works on two levels, as a 'kids-goofing-off movie,' and as an anthropological statement about American culture and mores" (Harmony Books, 1983, p. 29).

Synopsis of the Plot

The time is 1962; the place is Modesto, a town in California. All the action takes place during a single night in late summer between sunset and dawn.

The opening scene is at Mel's Drive-in, the local hamburger joint and hangout for teenagers. Two friends, Steve and Curt, are leaving town the next morning to go east to college. Steve leaves his car with another friend, Terry (Toad), who immediately decides to take up the favorite recreation of teenagers, cruising the main streets. Their other friend, John Milner, is a car mechanic who is noted as being the top drag racer in town and has never been beaten. The plot switches back and forth among these four friends and what happens to them on this night.

Steve and his girlfriend Laurie go to a school dance. Laurie doesn't want Steve to leave the next day and they fight over their relationship. Milner ends up with a twelve-year-old named Carol in his car, much to his disgust. He is also being pursued by Bob Falfa, who wants to race him. Curt is searching for a blonde in a white T-Bird who mouthed the words "I love you" and mysteriously disappeared. He finds himself coerced into joining members of the Pharaohs gang for part of the evening and even becomes an unwilling party to their pranks and lawbreaking. Toad picks up a girl, Debbie; and while they are off drinking and necking, the car is stolen.

Milner is finally able to take Carol home and helps Toad recover Steve's car. Laurie and Steve have split up and Laurie is picked up by Bob Falfa. Curt finally leaves the company of the Pharaohs and drives to the outskirts of town in search of the legendary Wolfman. Instead, he meets a fairly ordinary man who is eating popsicles and playing records. As the sun comes up, Milner and Falfa race and Falfa's car crashes. He and Laurie escape just before the car bursts into flames.

Laurie and Steve are reconciled, and Curt receives a phone call from the mysterious blonde.

Curt ultimately leaves to go to college, but Steve decides to stay. As Curt's plane takes off, the last thing he sees is a white T-Bird going down the road. As a postscript, Lucas tells what happens to each of the four friends, while a Beach Boys song heralds a new type of music unlike the traditional rock 'n' roll of the 1950s.

Ideas for Class Discussion

American Graffiti is a great film to discuss with teenagers since it is about high school students. What changes have occurred in teenagers' lives in the past 40 years? How have their social customs, such as dating or entertainment, changed? In 1962, young people were facing the beginning of the Vietnam era. What uncertainties do they face today?

Books and Materials Relating to This Film and Topic

Doherty, Thomas P. *Teenagers and Teenpics: The Juvenilization of American Movies in the 1950s.* Boston: Unwin Hyman, 1988.

Pollock, Dale. *Skywalking: The Life and Films of George Lucas.* New York: Harmony Books, 1983.

Other Media Resources for This Time Period

Back to the Future (1985, 116 minutes) Time travel movie about the 1950s

Big Night (1995, 109 minutes) Two Italian brothers try to save their failing restaurant by staging a huge feast to bring in customers. Rated **R**

Forrest Gump (1994, 142 minutes) This film, winner of the Oscar® for Best Picture, is sometimes seen as a metaphor for the baby boomers walking blindly through life. Low-I.Q. Forrest Gump meets with some of the most important people from the late 1950s through the 1970s.

Four Friends (1981, 115 minutes) Looks at the youth revolution of the 1960s; rated **R**

Invasion of the Body Snatchers (1956, 80 minutes) Sometimes regarded as a classic, this film deals with the issues of coercion, conformity, and the struggle against them during the 1950s. This version is preferred over the big-budget remake.

JFK (1991, 189 minutes) Oliver Stone's controversial film about New Orleans District Attorney Jim Garrison's quest to uncover the truth about the assassination of the president; rated **R**

The Last Picture Show (1971, 118 minutes) A look back at small-town America in the 1950s; a sequel called *Texasville* (1990, 126 minutes) explores the kinds of adult lives the major characters led. Rated **R**

Liberty Heights (1999, 127 minutes) The fourth of director Barry Levinson's Baltimore films, this movie explores the coming of age of some Jewish teenagers in the mid-1950s. Rated **R**

October Sky (1999, 108 minutes) True story of Homer Hickam, a West Virginia coal miner's son who is inspired by the Russian's launch of *Sputnik* to pursue rocketry

Peggy Sue Got Married (1986, 104 minutes) Time-travel movie that takes us back to the 1950s

Pleasantville (1998, 124 minutes) A back-to-the-future type movie in which two teenagers find themselves transported back to a 1950s town

Tucker: The Man and His Dream (1988, 110 minutes) Shortly after World War II, Preston Tucker tries to realize his dream to build a factory that produces the best cars ever made.

AMERICAN GRAFFITI

Universal Pictures, 1972; directed by George Lucas

Major Character	Actor/Actress
Curt Henderson	Richard Dreyfuss
Steve Bolander	Ron Howard
John Milner	Paul LeMat
Terry "Toad" Fields	Charlie Martin Smith
Laurie	Cindy Williams
Debbie	Candy Clark
Carol	Mackenzie Phillips
Disc Jockey	Wolfman Jack
Bob Falfa	Harrison Ford
Girl in Car	Suzanne Somers

WHAT TO WATCH FOR

This film was the first big hit for director George Lucas of *Star Wars* and *Indiana Jones* movie fame. It also was the first movie to capitalize on a growing sense of nostalgia for the "good old days" of the 1950s.

The action takes place in one single summer night in Modesto, California, in 1962. It tells of the adventures of four friends from high school, who have graduated and now must find their niche in the larger world.

This movie was very low budget and took only 28 days to shoot. The actors and actresses were mostly unknowns, and this movie proved to be their ticket to fame.

(continued)

Note the role of music in this movie. Wolfman Jack was a popular disc jockey of the late 1950s, a time in which music, particularly rock 'n' roll, separated the generations.

Critics believe that this movie portrays the last moment of American innocence before the country became engulfed in the Vietnam War and the domestic turbulence of the 1960s. The world of the teenagers, isolated from the outside, was one of cars, hamburger joints, and music. Even adults do not intrude very often in this movie. "Baby boomers," those born immediately after World War II ended, loved *American Graffiti*. It made a tremendous profit for Universal Studios and a millionaire of George Lucas. Many other films and TV shows set in the 1950s (*Back to the Future, Happy Days, Laverne and Shirley*) owe their inspiration to this movie and to the underlying desire to look back fondly at a time when life seemed much simpler.

Screening Notes

AMERICAN GRAFFITI

VOCABULARY

It seems that every period in history has a popular vocabulary all its own. While viewing this film, make a list of slang expressions used by the teenagers, such as "Holstein" for a police patrol car, and "J.D." for a juvenile delinquent. How do they compare with expressions used by teenagers today?

QUESTIONS BASED ON THE FILM

1. How are adults portrayed in the film?

   _____

   _____

   _____

   _____

2. Compare the amusements and diversions of teenagers in the early 1960s with those of teenagers today. Do you think that these were peculiar to California culture?

   _____

   _____

   _____

   _____

(continued)

3. Compare the high school hop in the film with dances held today.

_____

_____

_____

_____

4. We think of youth gangs as a new phenomenon. What were gangs like in the time that this movie portrays? How are they different today?

_____

_____

_____

_____

5. Are there still kids like Steve, Curt, Toad, and Milner today?

_____

_____

_____

_____

6. What happens to the four friends ultimately? Was this foreshadowed in any way?

_____

_____

_____

_____

— A TEACHER'S GUIDE TO FEATURE FILMS AND DOCUMENTARY SOURCES —

The Vietnam War has a plethora of media resources, but many are inappropriate for school use. This unit will present an annotated list of feature films that you may wish to view for your own education, some feature films that may be used in class, and documentaries relating to the Vietnam experience.

An asterisk (*) indicates that a film is appropriate for classroom use.

MEDIA RESOURCES FOR THIS PERIOD

Feature Films on Vietnam

China Gate (1957, 120 minutes) A "B"-Movie-Director Samuel Fuller film about American mercenaries in the French Foreign Legion during the French war in Indochina; Nat King Cole plays one of the soldiers, Lee Van Cleef plays the Viet Minh general, and Angie Dickinson is introduced to the public in this film. She plays a half-caste Vietnamese woman. The film makes a point about racial tolerance at the end.

The Quiet American (1958, 120 minutes) Note that the film turns Graham Greene's story of murderous naïveté on its head to make a point about the Cold War.

The Quiet American (2000, 100 minutes) Remake of the 1958 film; a love triangle set in the time of increasing United States involvement in Vietnam.

Saigon (1948, 94 minutes) The first post-World War II American film on Vietnam, it is a formula piece in which Saigon could be any mysterious locale.

Feature Films About Our Involvement in Vietnam and the Vietnam Era

Alamo Bay (1985, 85 minutes) This film tells the story of the clash between Vietnamese refugees and American workers whose jobs were threatened in a Texas fishing port. Rated **R**

Alice's Restaurant (1969, 111 minutes) Taken from Arlo Guthrie's song, it chronicles his problems with the local police and his draft board.

Apocalypse Now (1979, 150 minutes) Directed by Francis Ford Coppola and loosely based on Joseph Conrad's *Heart of Darkness* and Sir James Frazier's *The Golden Bough*, both written at the turn of the century; this film takes the Vietnam War into the realm of epic mythology. It has been written about and interpreted more than any other film about Vietnam. Rated **R**

The Big Chill (1983, 105 minutes) A group of yuppie friends reminisce about college in the sixties and how their lives have changed. Rated **R**

Billy Jack (1971, 112 minutes) One of several films about a renegade veteran who fights against bigotry and injustice on the home front; rated PG, it is in some ways a precursor to the first *Rambo* film that is set in the Pacific Northwest.

The Boys In Company C (1978, 126 minutes) A film that follows recruits from boot camp to combat in Vietnam; it is a transitional film in that, although the soldiers recognize the futility and corruption of the war, they continue fighting it for the sake of their unit's pride.

A Bright Shining Lie (1998, 118 minutes) Made-for-television movie about a career army man who is forced out of the military when he openly criticizes the way the war is being conducted; he returns to Vietnam as a civilian working with the army. Rated **R**

Coming Home (1978, 126 minutes) Film about a love triangle between a paraplegic Vietnam veteran, a marine officer, and his wife. Rated **R**

The Deer Hunter (1978, 183 minutes) The sprawling story of three steelworkers from Pittsburgh who join the Army and are captured by the Viet Cong; the Russian roulette episodes, which are unsubstantiated by the histories of the war, present the film's most riveting and controversial metaphors. The film, which won the Academy Award® for Best Picture, is rated **R.**

*Friendly Fire (1979, 145 minutes) The true story of two parents who are radicalized by the U.S. government's self-serving indifference to the death of their son in Vietnam

Full Metal Jacket (1987, 118 minutes) Stanley Kubrick's film about the training and combat action of soldiers in Hue during the Tet offensive. Rated **R**

Gardens of Stone (1987, 112 minutes) Francis Ford Coppola's film about the moral conflict felt by the soldiers of the Old Guard stationed at Fort Meyer, Virginia, in 1968, who comprise the burial detachment at Arlington Cemetery on the home front during the war; rated **R**

Getting Straight (1970, 124 minutes) Film that deals with the antiwar movement on U.S. campuses; it somewhat understates the movement's intellectual commitment, substituting for it hormonal drives and middle-class draft avoidance.

Good Morning Vietnam (1987, 120 minutes) Starring Robin Williams, story of an Armed Forces Radio DJ who angers his superiors in Saigon by his unorthodox actions; it is very loosely based on the experiences of Adrian Cronauer. Rated **R**

*The Green Berets (1968, 141 minutes) Typical John Wayne good guy/bad guy film with Wayne portraying a Special Forces commander; exemplifies the prowar attitude felt by many

Hair (1979, 121 minutes) Expatriate Czech director Milos Foreman's incisive adaptation of the late-sixties counterculture musical that sets its blackout numbers into a narrative line about a group of hippies, led by Treat Williams, who try to convince army recruit John Savage not to go to Vietnam; it serves as a kind of summary statement about the attitudes of the American public toward the war.

Hamburger Hill (1987, 110 minutes) Recreates the ten-day assault in May 1969 on a heavily fortified Viet Cong position on Dong Ap Bia, a mountain in the A Shau Valley; heavily covered by the media, including *Life* magazine, which published the photographs of 241 soldiers killed in the first seven days of the battle, Hamburger Hill was the last of the attrition battles as President Nixon's Vietnamization policy replaced the "meat-grinder" tactics of U.S. combat operations. At the end of the battle, the North Vietnamese retreated across the border into Laos and the Americans abandoned the mountain. Rated **R**

In Country (1989, 120 minutes) Story of a teenaged girl whose father was killed in action in Vietnam before she was born; when she tries to find out about her father in the war, she is rebuffed by Vietnam veterans. Rated **R**

The Iron Triangle (1988, 194 minutes) Shows the war through an American POW's growing understanding of his adversary; rated **R**

Jacknife (1988, 102 minutes) A troubled Vietnam vet and his relationship with his sister is threatened by her romance with an army buddy. Rated **R**

Kent State (1981, 180 minutes) A made-for-television movie based upon the student protests at Kent State University in Ohio on May 4, 1970; it focuses on the four students who were killed by the National Guard during the protests.

The Killing Fields (1984, 141 minutes) A true story about the destruction of Cambodia in the wake of the Vietnam War, told from the point of view of *New York Times* correspondent Sidney Schanberg and his Cambodian photographer/interpreter Dith Pran, whom he is forced to leave behind when the country falls to the Khmer Rouge; rated **R**

Kissinger and Nixon (1995, 90 minutes) A made-for-television movie about the attempts to untangle the United States from the tragedy of the Vietnam conflict

Nixon (1995, 191 minutes) An Oliver Stone film that features Sir Anthony Hopkins as the flawed president; rated **R**

The Path to War (2002, 140 minutes) Focuses on the time period 1964–66 and the initial phases of the escalation of the war under President Johnson

Platoon (1986, 120 minutes) Academy Award-winning film about the war in the jungles of Vietnam; many Vietnam veterans regard the atmosphere created by Vietnam veteran Oliver Stone in this film as the most accurate recreation yet of how the war actually felt, despite its monochromatic portrait of good and evil embodied in its two sergeant protagonists. Rated **R**

Rolling Thunder (1977, 99 minutes) A POW seeks revenge when thugs kill his wife and son; his revenge really takes on the wider role of seeking retribution for his Vietnam experiences. Rated **R**

A Rumor of War (1980, 200 minutes) A made-for-television movie based on Philip Caputo's novel, it follows a group of soldiers caught up in the horror and moral ambiguities of the war in Vietnam.

Summertree (1971, 88 minutes) A coming-of-age film with the Vietnam War as the backdrop

Trial of the Catonsville Nine (1972, 85 minutes) Dramatizes the trial of two Catholic priests, Daniel and Philip Berrigan, and seven others for antiwar and antidraft activities

We Were Soldiers Once . . . and Young (2002, 138 minutes) Based upon a book written by one of the combatants, this film focuses on the 1965 Battle of la Drang, one of the earliest significant conflicts in the war. Rated **R**

Who'll Stop the Rain (1978, 126 minutes) Based on Robert Stone's novel *Dog Soldiers* about how the lunacy of the war fed the domestic drug market and corrupted the institutions and relationships it was being fought to defend; rated **R**

A Yank in Vietnam (1964, 80 minutes) First combat film about Americans in Vietnam, and one of the few films actually shot in Vietnam; the plot revolves around the capture of a U.S. Army officer and a Vietnamese doctor by the Viet Cong.

Documentaries About the Vietnam Era
(Classroom Appropriate)

After 'Nam: CNN Special Report (1988, 30 minutes) Investigative report that looks at the effects of the Vietnam War

The Anderson Platoon (1967, 65 minutes) This Academy Award-winning French documentary follows a combat platoon during six weeks in the central highlands of Vietnam.

The Bloods of 'Nam (1986, 58 minutes) and *Remembering My Lai* (1989, 58 minutes) are two programs from the Public Broadcasting Service's *Frontline* series.

Dear America: Letter Home from Vietnam (1987, 84 minutes) Documentary produced for cable television that shows the Vietnam experiences of American soldiers through their letters

Hearts and Minds (1974, 112 minutes) Complex documentary that deals as much with American society as it does with the Vietnam War; winner of the Academy Award for Best Documentary Feature

In the Year of the Pig (1969, 103 minutes) Contains a history of French and American involvement in Vietnam

Television's Vietnam, Part 1 and Part 2 (1984, 116 minutes) A product of Accuracy in Media, it is basically a conservative response to the PBS series *Vietnam: A Television History,* but it uses many of the same techniques to sway audience opinion that it accuses the PBS series of using.

Vietnam: A Television History (1983, 60 minutes per episode) Thirteen-episode PBS series chronicles the Vietnam War; widely acclaimed, but not without its critics.

Vietnam—Chronicle of a War (1981, 89 minutes) Uses the CBS archives to document the history of the Vietnam War and traces our involvement year by year

Vietnam: The Ten Thousand Day War (1980, 49 minutes per episode) Thirteen episodes

The War at Home (1979, 100 minutes) Focuses on radical students at the University of Wisconsin and the antiwar movement in the United States

Why Vietnam? (1965, 32 minutes) Presents official U.S. government rationale used to justify air involvement in Vietnam

BOOKS RELATING TO MEDIA ON THE VIETNAM ERA

Adair, Gilbert. *Vietnam on Film: From* The Green Berets *to* Apocalypse Now. New York: Proteus Books, 1981.

Auster, Albert, and Leonard Quart. *How the War Was Remembered: Hollywood and Vietnam.* New York: Praeger, 1988.

Christensen, Terry. *Reel Politics: American Political Movies from* Birth of a Nation *to* Platoon. New York: Basil Blackwell, 1987.

Dittmar, Linda, and Gene Michaud, eds. *From Hanoi to Hollywood: The Vietnam War in American Film.* New Brunswick, NJ: Rutgers University Press, 1990.

Hellman, John. *American Myth and the Legacy of Vietnam.* New York: Columbia University Press, 1986.

Klein, Michael, and Peter Wiesner. "A Filmography of Oppositional Politics and Culture in the Vietnam Era, 1963–1974." *Historical Journal of Film, Radio, and Television* 11, no. 1 (1991): 59–72.

Rollins, Peter C., ed. *Hollywood as Historian: American Film in a Cultural Context.* Lexington, KY: University of Kentucky Press, 1983.

Rowe, John Carlos, and Rick Berg, eds. *The Vietnam War and American Culture.* New York: Columbia University Press, 1991.

Walsh, Jeffrey, and James Aulich, eds. *Vietnam Images: War and Representation.* New York: St. Martin's Press, 1989.

The End of the Twentieth Century

TEACHER'S GUIDE

NIGHTBREAKER

Symphony Pictures Corporation, 1988; directed by Peter Markle, color, 99 minutes

BACKGROUND OF THE FILM

Although the names are fictionalized, this movie provides a look back at a shocking episode in our nation's history: the use of U.S. soldiers as virtual guinea pigs at atomic test sites. During the 1950s, military planners considered nuclear weapons to be usable in close infantry support situations. Members of the 82nd Airborne, led by Corporal Russell Jack Dann (thinly disguised as Sergeant Jack Russell in the film), were brought onto the Nevada test site in 1957 for a series of experiments called Shot Smoky. In 1951, the army had formed a Human Resources Research Office (HUMRRO) to look at the psychological effects of atomic warfare. At Shot Smoky, HUMRRO psychologists wanted to know if soldiers who had witnessed an atomic detonation would be too shocked or panicked to complete their combat tasks. Second, they wanted to know if the soldiers' fear of radiation would impair their ability to perform in battle. The idea for the study, as explained in *Nightbreaker,* came from the Battle of Petersburg during the Civil War. Union troops had tunneled under the Confederate lines and loaded the tunnel with explosives. After the blast, the Union troops failed to act and just stood and gawked at the hole. HUMRRO wanted to find out if this would happen after an atomic explosion. Questionnaires were used to discover the soldiers' attitudes and knowledge about atomic bombs. This had all been tried before at test

sites in Nevada, so there is a question as to why yet another group of soldiers was exposed to atomic testing.

As shown in the film, pigs were used as test animals. To conduct an experiment called Test Priscilla, army uniforms were made for the pigs in order to test radiation on skin dressed in army clothes.

Some soldiers were given radiation film badges to wear to measure the dosage of radiation that they were receiving; however, these had not been proven to be accurate. It also appears that the U.S. Army changed the safe distance and radiation limit from test to test, and the soldiers were not told what exposure they were receiving. In attempting to conduct follow-up studies of these "atomic soldiers," many private researchers found that their army medical records and/or all records of their exposure to radiation had disappeared. The government has not acknowledged any correlation between illnesses suffered by the soldiers and their exposure to radiation.

SYNOPSIS OF THE PLOT

The plot of this film moves from 1988 back to 1956, intercutting between the experiences of Dr. Alexander Brown in both time periods.

Dr. Brown is in Las Vegas, Nevada, to receive an award as Neurologist of the Year. He is visited in his hotel room by a group of veterans and a man in a wheelchair. They want Brown to testify that he was part of an experiment, Project Nightbreaker, that sent soldiers close to an atomic detonation. Brown refuses.

The movie then flashes back to 1956, when Brown arrived in the Nevada desert to work with Dr. Roscoe Cummings. The place swarms with members of the media and spectators who applaud when the atomic bomb is detonated. Brown and Cummings are part of a project to interview soldiers about their attitudes toward nuclear warfare. The 76th Airborne is the group with whom Brown works. The supposed purpose of the project is to see if troops can witness an atomic blast and then take military advantage of it by seizing and securing objectives immediately after the blast.

Brown meets Sally Matthews, who is also working at the test site. Near the blast site, Matthews and Brown set up a model house typical of the time period, with dummies as inhabitants. At dawn, the soldiers are sent close to the blast site and are put in trenches. The debris from the explosion washes over the platoon. They are told to march to "ground zero," the actual point of detonation. The house and dummies are shown to be obliterated.

Back at camp, the soldiers and equipment are measured for radiation and then washed. Dr. Hatch, Matthews's boss, and Colonel Devereau, who is in charge of the experiments, argue over the use of soldiers at a site with so much radiation. Matthews tells Brown that the troops are being used as guinea pigs. Brown begins to question what he is doing. He goes into the files and finds out that his study has been done before and thus is being unnecessarily replicated.

The scene switches back to the present. A reporter keeps trying to pry into Brown's past. Brown's wife questions him about his experiences at the site. She is upset because she has always thought that their inability to have children was her fault.

Back at the test site in 1956, the soldiers are wrestling with test animals to get them into "radiation-proof" coverings. Later, the soldiers watch a film of the blast destroying the model house. By mistake, they are also shown the test animals being maimed by the blast and the radiation.

The soldiers prepare to go to a party at Sally Matthews's house, but when they arrive she refuses to let them in. She has learned that fallout from the last test blast has contaminated them.

Devereau warns Brown against fraternizing with the test subjects. Brown confronts him with changing the safe dosage level and lying to the soldiers.

Back in the present, Brown returns to the test site and remembers a time when he and the soldiers were moved to a point practically at ground zero. He remembers how the soldiers received the full force of the blast. At the dinner party where Brown has accepted his award, the veterans move into the room. Brown refuses to read his prepared remarks and decides to speak about his experiences at ground zero.

The movie ends with a final flashback of young Dr. Brown leaving the test site. Actual footage is then shown of soldiers at the site and the following words appear: "Between 1945 and 1962 over 235,000 servicemen and women were involved in above-ground atomic tests."

IDEAS FOR CLASS DISCUSSION

This film could lead to a class discussion about experimentation and the use of humans as guinea pigs. Is this ever justified? Should the rights of the individual ever be violated for the common good of the nation as a whole? And, of course, this film brings up the entire issue of nuclear safety, from weaponry to the use of nuclear energy. Today, soldiers from the Gulf War are complaining of various ills that they believe were caused by exposure to radioactive materials used in weapons. The threat of not only nuclear but also biological weapons is of great concern in the ongoing war against international terrorism.

BOOKS AND MATERIALS RELATING TO THIS FILM AND TOPIC

Boyer, Paul. *By the Bomb's Early Light: American Thought and Culture at the Dawn of the Atomic Age.* New York: Pantheon, 1985.

Browne, Corinne, and Robert Munroe. *Time Bomb: Understanding the Threat of Nuclear Power.* New York: William Morrow and Company, Inc., 1981.

Medvedev, Zhores. *Nuclear Disaster in the Urals.* New York: Random House, 1980.

Rafferty, Kevin, Jayne Loader, and Pierce Rafferty. *The Atomic Café.* New York: Bantam, 1982.

Rosenberg, Howard L. *Atomic Soldiers: American Victims of Nuclear Experiments.* Boston: Beacon Press, 1980.

OTHER MEDIA RESOURCES FOR THIS TIME PERIOD

Atomic Café (1982, 88 minutes) A documentary about the 15-year-long effort by the U.S. government to convince the public that nuclear war presented an acceptable level of risk

The China Syndrome (1979, 123 minutes) A film about potentially unsafe conditions in a civilian nuclear power plant

Coma (1978, 113 minutes) M.D.-turned-writer and director Michael Crichton's mystery about the intersection of biotechnology and amoral capitalism

Desert Bloom (1986, 106 minutes) A story about the strains on a Nevada family that are aggravated by the atomic tests nearby

The Insider (1999, 157 minutes) Based on the true story of a former tobacco executive who becomes an informant to expose unethical practices within the tobacco industry; rated **R**

Rage (1972, 104 minutes) George C. Scott's directoral debut in a film in which he stars as a sheep rancher whose son is exposed to chemical-weapons testing in the military; after the young man's death, his father sets out to identify those responsible.

Silkwood (1983, 131 minutes) A film biography of the plutonium plant worker and union activist who was killed in a car crash while en route to testify against the unsafe Kerr-McGee company that employed her; rated **R**

Played out into the future, these contemporary threats (and others) have caused filmmakers to imagine a range of alternative futures, some of which are

Mad Max Beyond Thunderdome (1985, 109 minutes) The only one of the *Mad Max* films with a PG-13 rating; sets its future in a postenergy-crisis environment

Soylent Green (1973, 97 minutes) Creates a future of overpopulation and food shortage

Testament (1983, 90 minutes) and *Planet of the Apes* (1968, 112 minutes) are examples of, respectively, near and distant postnuclear holocaust futures.

The End of the Twentieth Century

NIGHTBREAKER

Symphony Pictures Corporation, 1988; directed by Peter Markle

Major Character	Actor/Actress
Alexander Brown (past)	Emilio Estevez
Alexander Brown (present)	Martin Sheen
Sally Matthews	Lea Thompson
Sergeant Jack Russell	Joe Pantoliano
Paula Brown	Melinda Dillon
Dr. Roscoe Cummings	Paul Eiding
Colonel William Devereau	Nicholas Pryor
Dr. Hatch	Michael Laskin

WHAT TO WATCH FOR

This little-known film takes a look at a shocking episode in our nation's history: the use by the military of soldiers as guinea pigs at atomic test sites. The names are fictionalized, but the story is based on fact. Members of the 82nd Airborne (76th Airborne in the film), led by Corporal Russell Jack Dann (Sergeant Jack Russell in the film), were brought to Nevada in 1957 to participate in a series of experiments called Shot Smoky.

Note the carnival atmosphere of the spectator viewing area at the test site. It was considered a great privilege to be able to view an atomic bomb detonation. In nearby Las Vegas, advertisements based on atomic testing urged buyers to take advantage of "atomic bomb drops on high prices." The whole idea of having a test site nearby was looked upon as a moneymaker, a tourist draw. How does this relate to today's concerns about atomic power and to how people feel about having a nuclear power plant nearby?

(continued)

Note the questions Dr. Brown asks the soldiers as part of the experiment and the soldiers' naïveté about the atomic bomb and radiation. Also note the lecture that the soldiers are given about this experiment and how they will be perfectly safe. The radiation or film badge that is talked about was supposed to be worn by all soldiers to measure radiation; in reality, however, not all received a badge and the records of radiation dosage for those who wore badges have been either lost or destroyed. It is known that the army kept raising the safe-dosage limit during the course of the experiments. The army has not acknowledged any correlation between health problems suffered by soldiers and their involvement in exercises at the atomic test sites, although the army has acknowledged that soldiers were used as test subjects.

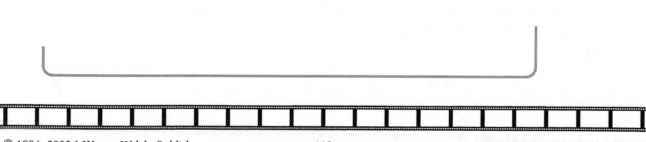

Screening Notes

The End of the Twentieth Century

NIGHTBREAKER

VOCABULARY

radiation

fallout

Geiger counter

ground zero

Atomic Energy Commission (AEC)

QUESTIONS BASED ON THE FILM

1. What is the atmosphere at the test site when the young Dr. Brown first arrives?

   _____

   _____

   _____

   _____

2. What are Sally Matthews' feelings about the bomb explosion and the spectators' reactions?

   _____

   _____

   _____

   _____

(continued)

3. What is the purpose of Project Nightbreaker?

_____

_____

_____

_____

4. When the soldiers are watching the film of the blast, how and why does their attitude change?

_____

_____

_____

_____

5. What do Dr. Hatch and Colonel Devereau argue about?

_____

_____

_____

_____

6. Why does Dr. Brown begin to change his mind about the necessity of the project?

_____

_____

_____

_____

Teaching Media Literacy Through Film

The OK Corral Gunfight—A Case Study

────────── TEACHER'S GUIDE ──────────

Films on historical subjects that are used in classes to bring a period, person, or event to life are rarely completely faithful to the facts they are recreating. Through reading, lecture, or discussion, teachers attempt to compensate for these inaccuracies, often relating them to the concerns or biases contemporary with the film's production with which its producers were trying to capture audience attention. But setting mere words against the multisensory immersion of a well-crafted film often leaves the teacher feeling less involved in teaching skills of visual literacy and interpretive sophistication than in confirming old misinformation.

To help students understand that there indeed is an interpretive structure embedded within each narrative and that current concerns do influence presentations of the past, "fire should be fought with fire." Time permitting, it is possible to teach these lessons in precisely this way. For producers—especially Hollywood producers—are loath to let a good story (especially a historical one, concerning familiar public figures) get away. As a result, there are a number of stories from U.S. history that have been filmed over and over again for an American public at different points in their development (enduring the Depression, fighting the antifascist crusade, confronting the Cold War, facing the New Frontier, or slogging through the Vietnam quagmire) by filmmakers with their own prejudices and concerns. Carefully selecting groupings of such films, showing them when teaching about the periods in which they were produced, and comparing their interpretations of the presented historical event with both accepted historical canon and each other, may result in students developing improved visual literacy skills, more sophisticated interpretive understanding, and a clearer recognition of how past and present are subtly interrelated.

A number of U.S. history topics lend themselves to this pedagogical technique. They include the Civil War, the expansion of the country at the expense of its native inhabitants, race relations, the nature and impact of immigration, the labor wars, the Depression, World War II and the decision to drop the atom bomb, the Civil Rights movement, and the Vietnam War. The films we have chosen to illustrate this technique are about an episode in the "civilizing" of the West that has entered the realm of mythology—the confrontation between the Earps and the Clantons at Tombstone, Arizona's OK Corral in 1881. At least eight theatrical films* have retold the story, beginning

* In addition, there has appeared a five-part version of the story as the concluding episodes of the long-running television series, *The Life and Legend of Wyatt Earp* (ABC Television, 1958–1961), which the audience was assured was faithfully recreated from the pages of the *Tombstone Epitaph* (though the audience was not told that the *Epitaph*—one of two Tombstone newspapers—was the mouthpiece of the Republican supporters of the Earp gang). David Wolper produced a documentary about the incident in his *Appointment With Destiny* series, called *Showdown at OK Corral* (1972). The town of Tombstone itself—"the town too tough to die"—daily recreates the gunfight (with the Earps as its clear heroes) to keep its tourist lifeblood flowing.

with *Law and Order* in 1932; yet none is very accurate when compared with what historians say actually happened there.

The three most famous renditions of the event were produced at important points in the United States' post-World War II history: John Ford's *My Darling Clementine* (1946) was made as Americans were readjusting their sights from beating the Axis to the challenges of reconversion at home and the "menace," both at home and abroad, of communism; John Sturges's *Gunfight at the OK Corral* (1957) was produced at the midpoint of the Eisenhower period of domestic conformity, organized crime revelations, juvenile delinquency, and Cold War confrontation in which the United States saw itself as the world's moral arbiter and global policeman; Pete Hamill's *Doc* (1971) appeared as Nixon's "positive polarization" was frustrating the Civil Rights movement and creating a society at war with itself at home, while the continuing Vietnam War fragmented the country. With careful investigation of each of the three films, paying close attention to not only the moral qualities of the main protagonists and the way in which the gunfight itself is characterized, but also the visualization of the towns in which the action takes place and their inhabitants, teachers can help students to understand the values and biases of the period in which each film was made. And when the films are compared to one another, issues of visual literacy (the ways in which sound, picture, and plot are manipulated to structure the audience's sympathy and understanding), historical interpretation, and the interaction of past and present (the uses the present makes of the past) appear in high contrast. Fire is indeed fought with fire.

Because of the complexity of this unit, more extensive background and plot synopsis material is being provided. Both because of time constraints and because the film *Doc* is emblematic of the rebellion against traditional values that characterized the 1960s—not only in its depictions of political authority, law enforcement, and American heroes, but also in its use of strong language and nudity—it may not

be suitable for high school use. The project will work just as well with the two earlier films, but if the sixties are to be included, the extensive plot summary included here will give students what they need to understand the film and to make the comparisons. From an operational standpoint, each film should be shown separately and students should be encouraged to carefully fill out the reproducible pages for it, not only to answer questions in discussion about that particular film, but as a memory aid to assist them in making the comparisons and reaching the conclusions about their similarities and differences later on.

BACKGROUND OF THE FILMS

In 1878, silver was discovered in the San Pedro Valley in southeastern Arizona. Within a year, territory that had previously been inhabited by Apaches and a few scrub ranchers, who eked out a living running cattle (their own and others') back and forth across the Mexican border, was overrun with miners hoping to make their fortunes and with others hoping to make their livings by serving the miners' needs. By 1880, the tent settlement of Tombstone that had been set up to service the miners was being gradually displaced by a permanent grid town. By the year's end, there were over three thousand claims and the extracting mills were producing a half-million dollars worth of bullion per month. A reservoir and conduit brought water into the town, a church was being built, and all manner of amenities were available. In addition to the hundred or so liquor sellers, restaurants, innumerable brothels, and gambling halls, Tombstone in 1881 had two banks, a fifty-room hotel, four theaters, four shoe stores, three clothing stores, two hardware stores, two blacksmiths, three livery stables, four lumberyards, and four meat markets. There were two newspapers, a photography studio, eight lawyers, two dentists, two druggists, and five physicians. The town also had a large Chinese section, referred to as "Hop Town," and a smaller segregated Mexican quarter. Chinese and Mexicans performed many of the menial and household chores of the town. Though Tombstone failed to attract the railroad, it would soon come to within 20 miles, making the town and its surrounding diggings both accessible and attractive.

Boomtowns like Tombstone were inherently unstable. The Apaches, embittered by the conditions of their captivity on the nearby San Carlos Reservation, were still a threat to settlers in that part of Arizona. The ranchers who controlled Cochise County found their power challenged by the miners and their town-based suppliers. In the resulting power struggle, the townsmen sought support from the Republican territorial administration, while the ranchers—who were called "cowboys" or "The County Ring"—identified themselves as Democrats. The townsmen sought law and order to protect and stabilize their prosperity and property, while the cowboys wanted to retain the older, more tolerant live-and-let-live system that had existed before the boom. The ready-made market for cattle, which the silver strike and the nearby San Carlos Indian reservation, with its military overseers, promised, drew the cowboys closer to Tombstone. By the end of 1877, N.H. "Old Man" Clanton and his sons Ike, Phin, Peter, and Billy had established a ranch 14 miles southwest of Tombstone. Newcomers Frank and Tom McLowery would establish themselves on a neighboring ranch. Gunman, killer, and sometime-lawman Johnny Ringo also drifted into the San Pedro Valley to join in the cross-border rustling.

It was into this volatile environment that the Earp brothers came between 1879 and 1881 with their common-law wives, children, and assorted associates. They would make their way as gamblers, saloon keepers, express guards, and sometime-lawmen. When need or profit demanded it, they were not averse to an occasional criminal act. James, the eldest; his brother Virgil, who worked most regularly as a lawman; and Wyatt, who had the most checkered career and the biggest reputation, came first. Morgan and Warren, the youngest, followed, and finally Wyatt's friend, the tubercular dentist-turned-gambler, John Henry "Doc" Holliday, arrived with his

volatile Hungarian-born mistress, "Big Nose" Katie Elder (or Fisher).

What happened in Tombstone in 1880 and 1881 remains a matter of controversy. The Earps became involved, mostly unsuccessfully, in Republican town politics. In 1881, Wyatt lost the Cochise County deputy sheriff's job to Democrat John Behan, with whom he was competing for the affection of a young actress named Josie (Sadie) Marcus, but got himself appointed deputy territorial marshal for southern Arizona by the Republican territorial authorities. In June 1881, Virgil was appointed to the job of town marshal and deputized his brothers. In March of that year, three men robbed a stagecoach of about $8,260 and killed its driver and a passenger. Doc Holliday (and, by implication, the Earps as well) was suspected in the affair. In a fit of anger, Katie Elder filed a deposition accusing Doc, and the Earps were seen carrying suspiciously heavy luggage on their frequent trips to visit their parents in California. The Earp supporters accused members of the cowboy faction of robbing the stage and of protecting the guilty. At one point Wyatt tried to enlist Ike Clanton's assistance in either bringing them to justice or silencing them permanently (depending on who is believed).

In the summer of 1881, Mexican forces ambushed and killed the patriarch of the Clanton family while he was on a cattle raid across the border. Shortly thereafter, yet another stagecoach was robbed. Charges flew back and forth between the Earp faction and the cowboy faction over who was responsible, and all sorts of minor insults and rumors fueled the animosity. The famous gunfight took place on October 26, 1881, after several days of name-calling and threats and the arrest and disarming of Ike Clanton by Virgil Earp. It took less than one minute and only some of the cowboys were armed. When the smoke cleared, Tom and Frank McLowery and Billy Clanton were dead. Virgil and Morgan Earp were seriously wounded and Doc Holliday was grazed by a bullet. Ike Clanton and Billy Claiborne survived the fight by fleeing from the scene. The controversy over the motives and responsibility for the fight began immediately thereafter in the newspapers, in the courts, and in a crescendo of vendettas that saw Virgil Earp wounded, Morgan shot and killed (a man of mixed race named Indian Charlie was among those charged), and the remaining Earps taking the law into their own hands. These controversies continue even today.

SYNOPSES OF THE PLOTS

MY DARLING CLEMENTINE

(Twentieth Century-Fox, 1946; directed by John Ford, 96 minutes)

In 1882, the Earp brothers—Wyatt, Morgan, Virgil, and James—are driving a herd of cattle across Arizona to California. They cross trails with "Old Man" Clanton and his sons, who offer to buy the herd from them. Wyatt refuses and talks to Clanton about going into Tombstone that night for "a shave, maybe . . . a glass o' beer." Leaving the youngest brother, James (who is engaged), to watch the cattle, the brothers ride into town where Wyatt's shave is interrupted by a drunken Indian shooting up the street. When the town marshal and his deputies refuse to confront Indian Charlie, Wyatt picks up a rock, distracts him, subdues him, and (literally) kicks him out of town. The mayor offers Wyatt the marshaling job, but Wyatt refuses. When the brothers return to their camp, they find James dead and the cattle gone. They return to Tombstone, and Wyatt becomes town marshal so that he can track down his brother's killers and so that "maybe when we leave this county, young kids . . . will be able to grow up and live safe."

Wyatt settles in and, while playing cards at the Oriental Saloon, encounters the Mexican woman Chihuahua and Doc Holliday. Doc is a former Boston surgeon with civilized manners, a tubercular cough, and a quick and theatrical temper. He owns the saloon and regards Wyatt with suspicion, though in several subsequent scenes he and Wyatt work together to maintain law and order. In one, the Clantons disrupt a theatrical performance by forcing the actor to go to a Mexican bar to declaim for them. Wyatt and Doc rescue the actor. Though Old Man Clanton apologizes to Wyatt, when the marshal leaves Clanton horse-whips his sons, telling them "when ya pull a gun, kill a man."

Doc's former fiancée, Clementine Carter, arrives in Tombstone, painfully reminding him of all he has lost. He rudely orders her to "go back home . . . where you belong," warning that "if you don't, I'm moving on." And to prove that he is no longer the man Clementine remembers, he offers to legitimize his relationship with Chihuahua. Partly out of concern for Doc and partly because of his own growing interest in Clementine, Wyatt tries to intercede with Doc, but this only makes things worse. The next morning, Clementine and Wyatt attend a church dance and the supper that follows. Doc appears and again orders Clementine to leave. After having words with Wyatt, Doc boards a stagecoach and, on its way out of town, throws Chihuahua some money. Understanding that this means good-bye, she rushes upstairs and tries to force Clementine to leave. Wyatt intervenes and in the fracas discovers that Chihuahua is wearing an engraved silver cross that James had bought for his fiancée. Chihuahua claims that Doc gave it to her and Wyatt, infuriated, sets out after Doc. He catches up with him and, against the stark majesty of Monument Valley, shoots Doc's gun from his hand. Together they return to Tombstone to confront Chihuahua.

Chihuahua admits that it was Billy Clanton, not Doc, who gave her the cross. She is shot in the back by Billy, who is spying on her through her window, to silence her. While Wyatt and Clementine convince Doc to operate on Chihuahua, Virgil chases Billy, mortally wounded in making his escape, back to the Clanton ranch. There he finds that Billy has died and, as he turns to leave the Clantons in their grief, Old Man Clanton shoots Virgil. Despite Doc's efforts to save her, Chihuahua also dies. Old Man Clanton rides into town, dumps Virgil's body on the street, and challenges Wyatt to come for them at the OK Corral.

At dawn the next day, Wyatt, joined by Morgan, Doc, and Tombstone's mayor and religious leader (who are left to guard the street), deliberately proceeds to the corral and demands that the Clantons "submit to proper authority." Ike Clanton begins shooting and is killed by Wyatt. Doc and Morgan have positioned themselves at the side of the corral. Doc reveals himself by coughing and is shot by Phin and Sam. Morgan then kills Sam, and Doc pulls himself back up and kills Phin, as he himself falls dead, leaving his white handkerchief fluttering from the corral railing. Old Man Clanton then surrenders, and Wyatt orders the apparently grief-stricken father to "start wandering." Clanton mounts his horse, but as he rides away, he draws a hidden pistol. Before he can fire, Morgan kills him with three fanned shots. From first shot to last, this rendition of the gunfight takes one minute and forty-five seconds. The film ends with Morgan and Wyatt leaving Tombstone. On the way out of town, they encounter Clementine. Morgan says good-bye and rides on. Clementine tells Wyatt that she is staying in Tombstone to start a school. Wyatt indicates that he may come east again and stop by to see her. The film ends with Wyatt riding off to join his brother.

GUNFIGHT AT THE OK CORRAL

(Paramount Pictures, 1957; directed by John Sturges, 122 minutes)

The film begins with three cowboys riding toward Fort Griffin, Texas, past the "boot hill" cemetery, to avenge the death of their leader's brother who drew on Doc Holliday. Kate Fisher, who saw the cowboys ride into town, goes to the hotel to warn Doc. She and Doc fight over his "airs," and Doc insists on keeping his "appointment with Mr. Bailey." She represents everything he loathes in himself, and he both despises and needs her. While Bailey and his friends wait for Doc in the saloon, U.S. Marshal Wyatt Earp rides into town on the trail of Ike Clanton who "has a dozen counts on him." But the town marshal, Cotton Wilson, has let Clanton slip through his fingers. Shocked by Wilson's apparent abdication of his responsibility, Wyatt goes to the saloon to pick up leads about Ike's plans. He is told that Doc Holliday played cards with Ike. Stopping momentarily to size up Bailey and his friends, Wyatt goes to the hotel to

make a deal with Holliday for information. Wyatt tells Holliday that Bailey has a derringer in his boot, but Doc refuses to help him, having been run out of several towns by Earp lawmen. Wyatt returns to the saloon and witnesses the confrontation between Doc and Bailey. Though Holliday kills Bailey in a fair fight, Marshal Wilson arrests him anyway and takes him to the hotel to await a lynch mob. Kate pleads with Earp to help Doc escape this fate and, against his better judgment, he does. Doc and Kate ride past the cemetery on their way out of town as Wyatt watches from his hotel window.

The scene then shifts to a stagecoach coming into Dodge City past its boot hill. (Note that all of these towns look alike and are peopled only by Caucasians.) The stage stops and a beautiful woman, Laura Denbo, gets off. Wyatt and Bat Masterson, who has come to borrow Wyatt's deputies to chase down Chief Dull Knife, who is "on a rampage," watch her and ask Wyatt's deputy, Charlie Bassett, who she is. Bassett is more concerned that "Doc Holliday and his lady are in town." Earp lends Masterson all of his deputies except Bassett, tells Masterson to have them back before the cattle drives reach town, and then goes off to confront Doc in a barbershop. After some discussion, Wyatt agrees to let Doc stay and gamble on condition that there would be "no knives, no guns, no killing."

That night, Bassett informs Wyatt that Miss Denbo is a professional gambler and that, against Wyatt's ordinance, she is playing in the main room. Aware that women in this position always cause trouble, Wyatt orders her to stop. But a drunken cowboy objects, and Wyatt, though himself unarmed, disarms him. He then arrests Miss Denbo for disturbing the peace. Though he offers to release her if she desists from gambling in public, she insists on going to jail. But on a bet, Doc persuades Wyatt to release her on condition that she confine her activities to a side room. Doc and she gamble the night away, while Kate feeds her jealousy with alcohol.

The next day, Wyatt gets word that "Richie Bell and two of his boys held up the bank at Salina, killed the cashier, and are heading this way." With his deputies away, Wyatt agrees to take Doc along, but refuses to deputize him. Together they kill the outlaws and cement their friendship. But when Doc returns, he has a coughing fit. He needs Kate, but she is nowhere to be found. Meanwhile, Wyatt begins courting Laura.

The next day, Doc demands that Charlie tell him where Kate is. Charlie resists and reminds Doc of his promise to Wyatt. But finally he reveals that Kate has taken up residence with Johnny Ringo across the "deadline" in the less respectable part of town. Doc confronts them but, mindful of his promise to Wyatt, refuses to accept Ringo's offer to fight him. Ringo calls him a coward and Doc leaves, as Kate silently expresses her anguish out of his sight.

That evening Wyatt offers to walk Laura home from a church dance and bazaar. While he is off courting her, an old enemy, cattle boss Shanghai Pierce, arrives with his men, including Johnny Ringo, to shoot up the town and teach Earp a lesson. When Charlie Bassett tries to stop them, he is wounded and the drovers invade and break up the dance. But their shooting interferes with Doc's winning streak at blackjack next door, and as Earp confronts Pierce and his men, Doc comes in behind them and takes their guns. When Ringo tries to draw on him, he shoots him in the arm and they are all carted off to jail by the citizenry. Wyatt thanks Doc and calls their debt even, but Doc insists that the tables are still not squared.

The next day Wyatt informs Doc that he and Laura are to be married and that he is quitting his job as a lawman. Doc wishes them well and returns to his hotel room. There Kate is waiting to beg him to take her back, but he says that it is too late for that. She leaves to return to Ringo, swearing that she will see Doc in hell for his rejection of her.

As Wyatt is packing up, Charlie brings him a letter from the attorney general offering him a job as U.S. marshal "whenever you want it" and a telegram from his brother Virgil. He reads it, and his whole demeanor changes. On the bluffs outside of town, he explains that he must respond to his brother's call for help. But Laura says that she cannot become a lawman's wife, following him from town to town,

waiting for the inevitable news that she is a widow. Wyatt rides off, leaving her there.

On Wyatt's way west, Doc Holliday joins him, looking, he says, for a healthier climate and a change of luck. The two arrive in Tombstone together, passing its boot hill. Doc checks in at the hotel, while Wyatt proceeds to his brother Virgil's house, where Virgil and Morgan and their families and Jimmie, the youngest brother who is engaged to be married, are awaiting his leadership. After dinner, Virgil lays out the situation. Ike Clanton has organized rustling into a big business and, with a corrupt county sheriff (Cotton Wilson) and judge, controls the county. But with the Earps in control of the city, Clanton can't ship his cattle. Virgil is troubled by Doc's presence in Tombstone; Wyatt defends his presence as his responsibility. Wyatt "shuts the town to trouble" by banning firearms within its limits. He then accepts the marshal's commission, offered earlier, thus superseding the sheriff's power. While Wyatt is waiting for his marshal's commission, he and John Clum's citizen committee turn the Clanton gang away from an Eddie Foy performance at the Schieffelin Theater. At the same time, Kate Fisher arrives in town and is taken to the Clanton ranch by Johnny Ringo, who taunts Doc almost into violating his promise to Wyatt. In stopping him, Virgil advises Doc to get out of Wyatt's life. Doc does in fact decide to leave and bids farewell to Wyatt.

The next day the youngest Clanton, Billy, is arrested for drunkenness. At the same time, Wyatt receives his appointment as U.S. marshal. He decides to take Billy home and simultaneously confront Ike with this new situation. The Clantons' mother chides her son and tells Wyatt that "I don't know what I'm going to do with that boy. The way he's going now, he's going to end up like his father, shot down for stealing cattle." Wyatt then talks to the boy about living up to older brothers' reputations, and Billy confides to Wyatt that "It's not that I want to be a gunfighter exactly, it's just—I don't know, sometimes I get lonely." Billy then promises to repent. As Wyatt leaves, Ike and Cotton Wilson ride up and make threatening noises, but when Wyatt shows them his marshal's appointment, Ike backs off and again offers him a bribe, which Wyatt rejects. Ike then holds a meeting of his gang and decides to kill Wyatt that evening, forcing the rest of the Earps into a family feud. Kate overhears their plot.

That night Jimmy replaces Wyatt on rounds and is killed in his place. Wyatt finds the body and, despite Doc's warning, vows revenge: a personal fight. For his part, Doc finds Kate and forces her to reveal the names of the killers. He then lunges for her but collapses in a tubercular spasm. Kate flees for her life but is drawn back, believing that Doc is dying. Still later, Billy brings a message from Ike to Wyatt telling him to meet the Clanton gang (Ike, Phin, and Billy Clanton; Frank and Tom McLowery; and Johnny Ringo) at sunup at the OK Corral. Wyatt tells Billy not to join in, but Billy says he must be loyal to his brothers. Wyatt says he understands. Waiting at Virgil's house for sunup, Virgil's wife chastises the Earp brothers for not behaving as lawmen and for rejecting the help of the citizens' committee. Wyatt then goes to Doc's hotel, desperate for his help, but finds him unconscious and watched over by Kate. He returns to his own room filled with despair, staring into the mirror at what he has become.

At dawn, the Clantons ride from their ranch while their mother waits in dread. Doc awakens and, despite Kate's pleas, determines to stand "with the only friend I've ever had." The gang arrives at the OK Corral, where they are met by Cotton Wilson, who is sent to try to get Wyatt to meet Ike alone. The Earps and Doc Holliday assemble and begin walking toward the corral. Wilson stops them and delivers his message, but is accused by Doc of being in on Jimmy's killing. Wyatt tells Cotton to get back with his friends. Cotten reports to Ike and asks to be let out. Ike tells him to stand by the horses, but when the gunplay starts, he tries to flee and is shot in the back by Ike. The gunfight begins when Frank McLowery opens fire from his hiding place in a wagon. During its course, Morgan is shot by Phin Clanton, who is, in turn, shot by Doc as he rescues Morgan. Wyatt then sets the wagon alight by shooting a kerosene lamp hanging

from it, and Frank McLowery is set afire. In an attempt to save him, his brother Tom charges Wyatt and is killed by him at close range. Virgil is then shot in the leg by Ike as he attempts to move forward. Wyatt rescues Virgil, and when Ike tries to kill the distracted Wyatt, the latter blows him apart with a shotgun blast. Ringo and Billy Clanton try to flank Doc from different sides, and Billy grazes Doc in the right arm. Wyatt then wounds Billy in the shoulder, but he crawls away. Doc then sees Ringo sneaking behind the horses and, despite his wound, tells Wyatt that "I'll take care of Ringo." Wyatt checks his brothers and sets out after Billy. After some hide-and-seek, Doc kills Ringo with three shots. Grievously wounded, Billy runs down Allen Street to Fly's Photographic Gallery with Wyatt in hot pursuit. Billy breaks in and staggers upstairs to a balcony. Wyatt follows, ordering Billy to give up. Wyatt enters the gallery and Billy wildly shoots at him. Wyatt is unable to fire back, but before Billy can steady his aim, Doc fatally shoots him from outside through the window. Billy tumbles over the balcony and falls dead at Wyatt's feet. Surveying the carnage, Wyatt drops his gun, takes off his badge, and drops it to the ground. The gunfight took exactly seven minutes in this version.

In the gunfight's aftermath, Wyatt comes to the saloon to thank Doc. He says he is going to California to try to find Laura. Doc returns to the gaming table. Wyatt rides past boot hill and off into the frame as the film ends.

Doc

United Artists, 1971; directed by Frank Perry, 122 minutes)

Out of a dusty, windswept desert night, a lone weary rider (Doc Holliday), dressed in black, approaches a run-down Mexican cantina. Inside are a Hispanic bartender, two cowboys playing cards, and a prostitute (Katie Elder). He plays poker with the cowboys (one of whom is Ike Clanton, the other his nephew known only as "the Kid") for the lady's "services." The stranger wins and, after spending the night with the prostitute, reluctantly agrees to take her to Tombstone. He tosses some coins on the ground to pay the Mexican for providing them with provisions for the trip, and the Mexican curses them under his breath. Halfway across the desert, they discover that he has filled the canteen with vinegar. They barely make it to the mountains, but, refreshed there, enter Tombstone in style the next morning.

The town is a raucous place, filled with all manner of people—Anglos, Mexicans, Asians, Indians—of all classes and occupations. Katie Elder is welcomed into a brothel and Doc collapses in his hotel room. The door to his room swings open and a menacing figure enters, rousing Doc. He smiles and embraces his friend Wyatt Earp. The scene shifts to a smoky Alhambra Saloon where the Clantons are drinking. Earp and Doc enter and exchange words. Wyatt then explains the situation in Tombstone. "It's wide open. . . . So you organize the gambling . . . I'll run the law, we'll both end up rich, very rich." Katie enters and Ike accosts her. Wyatt intercedes and pistol-whips Ike. The cowboys, except for Ike's nephew, the Kid, leave, but Johnny Ringo warns him to watch himself—"that Wyatt Earp ain't right in his head." Holliday interrupts his gambling, asks the Mexican band to play a waltz, and proceeds to dance with Katie, as a concerned Wyatt looks on.

The scene shifts again to Wyatt's house the next day. Virgil and Morgan Earp are wrestling on the ground while Wyatt, his common-law wife, Mattie, and Virgil's wife, Alie, prepare for a political reception. As Wyatt politics for sheriff, off-camera voices explain the relationship between Doc and Wyatt and refer to Doc as Earp's "heavy artillery." Doc is introduced to Wyatt's political opponent, Johnny Behan, and to a skeptical John Clum, editor of the *Tombstone Epitaph;* but as Clum questions him, Doc breaks into a coughing fit and is helped away by Wyatt, who directs him to a "Chinaman" at the end of Allen Street, where he gets high on opium. Upon leaving the opium den, Doc encounters the Kid, who asks him to teach him how to shoot. Doc reluctantly agrees and gives him a

lesson the next day, telling him the story of his life in the process.

Back in town, Wyatt and Ike again collide. That night Doc has another coughing fit and, concluding that he must do something to change his life, steals Katie from her brothel and sets her up in a small cabin at the edge of town, which she fixes up for the two of them. Domestic bliss ensues, despite the evident disapproval of the arrangement by Wyatt and such "respectable" town dwellers as Alie Earp, who visits Katie in a later scene to advise her to "go to church."

A stagecoach rolls into town with doors flapping and a wounded guard in the box. Wyatt rides to get Doc to join in the search for the holdup men, who stole $80,000 in gold from the stagecoach. After saying good-bye to Katie, they find the empty strongbox on the trail and, guessing that Johnny Ringo is responsible, follow tracks toward the Clanton ranch. At the same time, the Kid informs Ike of the robbery. Ike, too, concludes that Ringo is the culprit and that he will bring the law down on all of them. Earp and Holliday ride in. Words are exchanged as Ike tells Wyatt that "We don't steal money." Surrounded by Clanton and McLowery men, Ike challenges Earp to a fistfight and beats him severely until Doc stops it. Doc tends his friend's injuries, and Wyatt tells him, "I'm gonna kill him." Doc returns with a battered Wyatt to Wyatt's house and, as Doc returns to Katie and domestic bliss, Virgil tells Wyatt that Wells Fargo has offered a $20,000 reward for the stagecoach robbers. Wyatt sends Virgil to set up a meeting with Ike. He plans to offer Ike the reward in return for the bandits. "Ike gets some money," Wyatt says ominously, "we get the credit, then we win the election and we clean up Tombstone," to which Virgil responds, "You mean, clean out Tombstone."

The next day as Wyatt arrests some drunks fighting, Doc and Katie go for a ride in the country. Later, John Clum encounters Doc in the barbershop and asks him why Wyatt wants to be sheriff. Clum suggests that money is the reason. When Doc demurs that Johnny Behan hasn't gotten rich from the job, Clum says that this is because Behan is "dumb and honest." When Doc asks Clum if he thinks that Wyatt is honest, Clum answers, "Nope." Just then, shots ring out across the street. Doc, to his horror, discovers that the Kid has shot a man who drew on him. When Wyatt tries to arrest the Kid, Doc turns on him and Sheriff Behan takes the Kid into custody. Earp looks at his friend in shocked bewilderment.

That night Johnny Behan and Wyatt Earp make speeches at a town rally. Behan talks as a permanent resident of the town and is applauded. Earp responds that he, too, is in Tombstone to stay, and tells his audience that "there is only one way to get rid of the gun [to ensure stability and prosperity] and that is to use the gun. . . . I hope you'll let me get the job done for us, for all our families. . . . I hope you all get home safe." Wyatt and Clum discuss what he (Wyatt) and Doc are after. Clum concludes that while Wyatt wants to win, Doc is searching for something to make his life worthwhile—"some gesture of size."

Later that night, the Earps and the Clantons meet on the trail. Wyatt tells Ike that he needs Ringo before the election. When Clanton refuses to help Wyatt win an election that might result in his own death, Wyatt blackmails him by telling him that the Kid is in jail and may be charged with murder if Ike doesn't cooperate. Meanwhile, Doc bails out the Kid. After his release, the Kid tells Holliday that his ambition is "to be just like you" and, in shock, Doc begins to recognize the monster he is creating. When he returns home, Katie asks him for a long-term commitment and Doc recoils in confusion. As Katie reminds him of his mortality, he begins to cough and runs away.

The next morning, Virgil informs Wyatt that Doc has bailed out the Kid. Wyatt concludes that the deal is now ruined and that the Clantons must now be killed to silence them. He goes to Doc's house to get him, but Katie doesn't know where he is. Wyatt accuses Katie of changing Doc—of beguiling him sexually. Wyatt finds Doc at the Alhambra, drunk and asleep. Doc greets him with the Spanish phrase "Buenos días, Señor Muerte" (Good morning, Mr. Death). Wyatt tells Doc that there will now be trouble with the Clantons, but Doc responds that Wyatt's

trouble is no longer his, that he is sick to death of killing, and that he wants "to leave something behind." Wyatt walks away.

That night, Wyatt plots with his brothers to incite the Clantons into a gunfight. By threatening to bring robbery, conspiracy, murder, and attempted bribery charges against Ike and the Kid, Wyatt plans to force the Clantons to come after him so that he can kill them in self-defense. Virgil and Morgan go off to tell Billy Clanton. A distraught Katie appears and begs Wyatt to help her find Doc. Wyatt suggests that she look for him at "the Chinaman." When she finds him, she berates him and burns the place down. High on opium, Doc tells Katie that they might go away together soon. But Katie, disgusted with him, walks away and Doc turns back to the fire.

The next morning, the Clantons and McLowerys ride toward Tombstone. They send the Kid ahead to scout the situation. Wyatt swears in his brothers, now wearing suits, as deputy marshals. The Kid finds Doc at breakfast and explains why the Clantons and McLowerys are coming in. He tells Doc that he will be one of the seven and that he doesn't want to have to kill him. Doc then has his picture taken at Fly's studio, returns to his shack where Katie is packing, and without saying anything, leaves to join the Earps who are arming themselves with pistols and shotguns at the Alhambra. Wyatt and Doc stare at each other, then they walk out onto the street.

The Clantons and McLowerys arrive at the OK Corral where they meet the Kid. Sheriff Behan warns them about gunplay within the town limits, says he doesn't want any trouble, and orders them to give up their guns. Ike refuses and tells Behan to "tell it to the . . . marshal." Behan then tries to stop the Earps, telling them that the town is his jurisdiction. Earp replies that they can "settle it in court." Clum advises Wyatt that this gunplay will settle nothing, to which Earp responds that "you'd be surprised things you can settle with a gun." And Doc and the three Earps, with shotguns in hand, march towards the corral. Seeing the shotguns, the cowboys spread out. Doc and the three Earps enter the corral, and spread out themselves. Ike tells Holliday that this is none of his affair and that they've come to talk. At this point the Earps start firing. Ike and Frank McLowery are hit with the first blast, Billy falls a second later, and a second McLowery is killed by Doc. The Kid draws his pistol and shoots Morgan Earp. Ike tries to get off a shot and Wyatt shoots him with his Buntline special. The Kid and Doc aim at one another, but the Kid relents and holsters his gun, at which point Doc shoots him through his heart. The whole affair takes 20 seconds.

Doc and Wyatt scan the carnage while Virgil announces that Morgan is dead. As a crowd gathers, Doc walks away, half stunned. Wyatt watches him leave and then speaks to the crowd: "They killed my brother; they came to try to destroy everything that we've been trying to build together. But I'm telling you that my brother's death is not going to be in vain, 'cause from this we're going to build a better town— we're going to build a better Tombstone. I swear that to you." The crowd applauds as Virgil looks on incredulously. Doc gets his horse and meets Wyatt on the way out of town. "Why the Kid?" Wyatt asks. Doc responds, "I guess he reminded me of too many things." The movie ends as he rides away, the street dissolving to the photograph he had taken earlier that day with his name and dates: John H. Holliday, 1852–1887.

BOOKS AND MATERIALS RELATING TO THIS TOPIC

Faulk, Odie B. *Tombstone: Myth and Reality.* New York: Oxford University Press, 1972.

Lyons, Robert, ed. *My Darling Clementine: John Ford Director.* New Brunswick, NJ: Rutgers University Press, 1984.

Marks, Paula Mitchell. *And Die in the West: The Story of the OK Corral Gunfight.* New York: Simon and Schuster, 1989.

AN EARP FILMOGRAPHY

1. *Law and Order* (1932)

2. *Badmen of Arizona* (1935)

3. **Frontier Marshal* (1939)

4. **My Darling Clementine* (1946)

5. *Gunfight at the OK Corral* (1957)

6. *Cheyenne Autumn* (1964)

7. *Hour of the Gun* (1967)

8. *Doc* (1971)

9. *Sunset* (1988), rated **R**

10. *Tombstone* (1993), rated **R**

11. *Wyatt Earp* (1994)

* Claims to have used Wyatt Earp as a source

Note: Wyatt Earp supposedly appears as an extra in Alan Dwan's *The Half-breed* (1916) starring Douglas Fairbanks. Among the pallbearers at Earp's funeral in 1929 were Western film stars Tom Mix and William S. Hart.

MY DARLING CLEMENTINE

Producer: Samuel G. Engel, Twentieth Century-Fox (1946, 96 minutes)

Director: John Ford

Writers: Samuel G. Engel and Winston Miller from the story by Sam Hellman, based on *Wyatt Earp, Frontier Marshal* by Stuart N. Lake and the reminiscences of Wyatt Earp as told to John Ford

Cinematographer: Joseph P. MacDonald

Major Character	Actor/Actress
Wyatt Earp	Henry Fonda
John "Doc" Holliday	Victor Mature
Chihauhua	Linda Darnell
Clementine Carter	Cathy Downs
"Old Man" Clanton	Walter Brennan
Virgil Earp	Tim Holt
Morgan Earp	Ward Bond
James Earp	Don Garner
Billy Clanton	John Ireland
Ike Clanton	Grant Withers
Sam Clanton	Micky Simpson
Phin Clanton	Fred Libby
Granville Thorndike	Alan Mowbray
Mayor	Roy Roberts
Kate Nelson	Jane Darwell

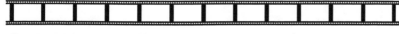

GUNFIGHT AT THE OK CORRAL

Producer: Hal Wallis, Paramount Pictures (1957, 122 minutes)

Director: John Sturges

Screenplay: Leon Uris from an article by George Scullin, with sound track including "Gunfight at the OK Corral" sung by Frankie Laine

Major Character	Actor/Actress
Wyatt Earp	Burt Lancaster
Doc Holliday	Kirk Douglas
Laura Denbow	Rhonda Fleming
Kate Fisher	Jo Van Fleet
Ike Clanton	Lyle Bettger
Johnny Ringo	John Ireland
Cotton Wilson	Frank Faylen
Charlie Bassett	Earl Holliman
Shanghai Pierce	Ted DeCorsia
Billy Clanton	Dennis Hopper
John Clum	Whit Bissell
John Shaussey	George Mathews
Virgil Earp	John Hudson
Morgan Earp	DeForest Kelley
James Earp	Martin Milner
Bat Masterson	Kenneth Tobey
Ed Bailey	Lee Van Cleef
Betty Earp	Joan Camden
Mrs. Clanton	Olive Carey
Mayor Kelley	Nelson Leigh
Tom McLowery	Jack Elam

Teaching Media Literacy Through Film

--- **Doc** ---

Producer: Frank Perry, United Artists (1971, 122 minutes)
Director: Frank D. Gilroy, Frank Perry
Screenwriter: Peter Hamill
Production designer: Gene Callahan
Cinematographer: Gerald Hirschfield

Major Character	Actor/Actress
Dr. John Holliday	Stacy Keach
Wyatt Earp	Harris Yulin
Katie Elder	Faye Dunaway
Ike Clanton	Mike Witney
The Kid	Denver John Collins
John Clum	Dan Greenberg

The OK Corral Gunfight—A Case Study

QUESTIONS BASED ON THE FILM

1. What are the characteristics of the West shown in the film? What does it symbolize? Think about the town itself, what its construction materials are, what the interiors look like, and whether certain kinds of things happen in particular places in answering the question.

_____

_____

_____

_____

_____

2. What kind of people are Wyatt and his brothers? What values do they represent?

_____

_____

_____

_____

3. What kind of people are the Clantons? What motivates their actions?

_____

_____

_____

_____

(continued)

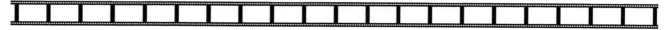

4. What kinds of people are portrayed in the film? Think about the ethnic and racial composition of the population, the costumes they wear, and whether certain kinds of people play certain kinds of roles in the film as you answer.

_____

_____

_____

_____

5. What kind of person is Doc Holliday in the film? What motivates him?

_____

_____

_____

_____

6. What roles do women play in the film? What does the film tell you about a woman's place?

_____

_____

_____

_____

7. In the film, Doc is torn between the values of his past life in the East and his current situation. How is this struggle portrayed in the film?

_____

_____

_____

_____

(continued)

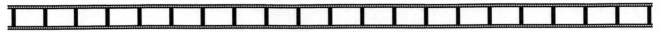

8. How is the relationship between Wyatt and Doc explained in the film? How is their cooperation and friendship justified?

_____

_____

_____

_____

_____

9. What causes the gunfight to happen in the film? What motivates the two sides to confront one another in this way?

_____

_____

_____

_____

_____

10. Who is right and who is wrong in the film? Why?

_____

_____

_____

_____

_____

The OK Corral Gunfight—A Case Study

FILM COMPARISON SHEET

1. How do the films' portrayals of the West in the early 1880s differ from one another? How might you explain these differences?

   _____

   _____

   _____

   _____

2. How does the portrayal of the Earps change? What does this tell you about how our perceptions of ourselves and our heroes have changed over these decades?

   _____

   _____

   _____

   _____

3. How do the portrayals of the Clantons and their motivations change? What does this tell you about the country's images of villainy at the times these films were made?

   _____

   _____

   _____

   _____

(continued)

4. What differences exist in the portrayals of the people and their roles in the films? What does this say about our consciousness of and sensitivity to racial and ethnic diversity and stereotypes when each of these films was made?

_____

_____

_____

_____

5. How do Doc's personality and motives change in the films? When Doc is compared to the Clantons, what can be learned about perceptions of good and evil in the world at the time each film was made?

_____

_____

_____

_____

6. By comparing women's roles in the films, what changes occurred with respect to the filmmakers' perceptions of "a woman's place" over these decades?

_____

_____

_____

_____

7. How does Doc's inner struggle change in the different films? What does his treatment of the women in his life tell us about a man's psyche at the times these films were made?

_____

_____

_____

_____

(continued)

8. How does the Wyatt–Doc relationship change among films? Does this justification help us to understand such things as America's cooperation with Stalin against Hitler in World War II, or the country's willingness to put up with dictators in the struggle against communism during the Cold War?

_____

_____

_____

_____

9. How do notions of personal greed, community, duty, and family loyalty as motivating factors change in the films? How are these valued as the Earps and the Clantons collide in each film?

_____

_____

_____

_____

10. How do our ideas of heroism and villainy change among the films? What does this tell us about the time in which each film was made?

_____

_____

_____

11. Which of the films most accurately tells the story of the gunfight at the OK Corral? Why?

_____

_____

_____

_____

Film Analysis Guide Sheet

1. Title of the film _____

2. Date of production _____

3. Studio _____

4. Director _____

5. **Major character**   **Actor/Actress**

   _____   _____

   _____   _____

   _____   _____

   _____   _____

   _____   _____

   _____   _____

   _____   _____

   _____   _____

   _____   _____

   _____   _____

6. Historical event portrayed by the film _____

7. Approximate dates covered by the film _____

8. Are any historical consultants listed in the credits? If so, who? _____

   _____

   _____

(continued)

9. Synopsis of the plot _____

_____

_____

10. Does this film portray the historical event or time period accurately? If so, how? (Note costuming, sets, scenery, props, manners, etc.)

_____

_____

_____

_____

11. How does this film deviate from the historical facts, or, in other words, what inaccuracies can you find in this film?

_____

_____

_____

_____

_____

12. What cinematic devices (fades, dissolves, flashback, montage, split scene, bridging shots, etc.) did the filmmaker use to convey a meaning or feeling in this film? Give examples.

_____

_____

_____

_____

_____

(continued)

13. What underlying message(s) does this film contain? Explain.

_____

_____

_____

_____

14. In your opinion, of what use is this film in explaining or illuminating a historical event, figure, or time period?

_____

_____

_____

_____

15. Research a particular aspect of the film. How does the historical research and evidence support or conflict with the film? Why do you think the filmmaker(s) chose this particular portrayal? If you were making the film, how would you stage it? Why?

_____

_____

_____

_____

_____

_____

_____

Glossary of Common Film Terms

actuality footage: Film or video that is not set up and/or dramatized; e.g., newsreel film

aspect ratio: The ratio of the horizontal to the vertical in TV or film; film has an aspect ratio of 6 hortizontal units to 4 vertical units while television has an aspect ratio of 4 by 3. This is what necessitates letter-boxing a film to make it fit a television screen without distortion.

audio: The sound in a film or broadcast

backlighting: Using the main source of light behind a subject to silhouette the figure

black comedy: Comedy that deals with macabre topics such as murder or nuclear war; *Dr. Strangelove* is a good example.

bridging shot: Shot that covers a jump in place or time, such as newspaper headlines, falling leaves, hands of a clock, or an airplane taking off

camera angle: Angle at which a camera is pointed at a subject; a high-angle shot from above a subject can make the subject look small. A low-angle shot can make a subject look large.

cinematography: The art and science of motion picture photography; *videography* is a term used to describe video photography.

close-up: Any close shot, usually of a subject's face

credits: The list, usually at the end of a film, of the crew and cast of a production

cut: The instantaneous switch from one image or scene to another

crosscutting: Cutting between two or more scenes to portray parallel action—events that are occurring simultaneously

dissolve: To fade out one image while fading in another

docudramas: Historical events that are reenacted, often in fictionalized versions; for example, *Roots, Holocaust*

documentary: Film that is generally, but not always or completely, not fictional, usually containing actuality footage, interviews, and a narration; *documentary* is an elastic term that may include reenactments, still pictures, sound effects, stock footage, graphics, and/or interpretive materials.

dolly shot: Shot taken with a camera moving on wheels (called a dolly); also called a follow or tracking shot

DVD: digital video disc; more and more films are coming out on DVD, which gives a clearer image and allows the viewer to access certain parts of the films without forwarding and rewinding.

editor: The person who cuts and splices together the film into its final form; editors in video do this electronically with computerized equipment.

establishing shot: A wide shot that establishes the location of a scene for the viewer

fade-in/-out: In a fade-in, the screen gradually changes from black to the image. In a fade-out, the image dissolves to black.

flashback: A scene that is brought into the film from the past; sometimes almost an entire film can be a flashback from the present to the past, as in *Little Big Man*.

focus: The clarity or sharpness of an image

(continued)

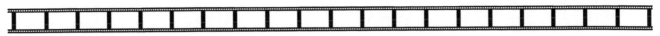

American History on the Screen

Glossary of Common Film Terms (continued)

foley: A largely manual process for introducing any nonmusical or nonspoken sound effect or noise as part of the postproduction process

freeze frame: Stopping of an individual frame to give the impression of a still image or photograph

gaffer: The chief electrician in a production; the *best boy* is the gaffer's assistant.

genre: The type of a film, such as science fiction, Western, or horror film

grip: The person in charge of props, sometimes called the key grip

letter boxing: The technique of compressing a film horizontally and enclosing it in black on the top and bottom of the screen to make it fit on a television screen without distortion

mise-en-scène: What actually takes place on the set—the actors, direction, type of cameras, etc.

montage: (1) the editing of film; (2) editing shots together in such a way as to produce a total meaning different from the parts actually shown

narrative: The story of a film

over-the-shoulder shot: Shot used in interviews or dialogue in which the camera is placed behind and to the side of one of the speakers to show a portion of his or her head and shoulders as well as the other speaker

pan: The horizontal movement of the camera lens from left to right or right to left

pan and scan: In a film produced on DVD for use on a consumer television set, to show the reactions of two main characters who may be standing far apart from each other, a technique is used where first a close up of one and then a close up of the other is shown superimposed over the scene. This is to compensate for the small screen on a television set and its smaller aspect ratio.

point-of-view shot: Also called a subjective shot, a shot that shows the scene from the point of view of one of the subjects

reverse angle: A shot taken from the opposite side of a subject from that previously shown, often to show a second person in a dialogue

scene: A coherent segment of the film, made up of a number of shots, that takes place in one location and at one time period and usually revolves around one particular action

sequence: A section of film containing a group of scenes that constitutes a more or less complete thought, very often beginning and ending with a cut, dissolve, or fade

shot: A single unedited piece of film or video that is taken by a camera

split screen: Section of film with two or more distinct images on the screen that are not super-imposed and do not overlap

stock footage: Film or video shot for one purpose but used for another, usually used as background or establishing material

tilt: The vertical movement of the camera lens up and down

videography: See cinematography.

voice-over: Narration in which the narrator is not seen, used often in documentaries and TV commercials

wipe: An effect where one image pushes or "wipes" another image off the screen; wipes can have many shapes and are used more in TV than in film.

zoom: Changing the focal length using the special lens of the camera to go from wide angle to telephoto or vice versa

Video Sources

A&E Home Video, P. O. Box 2284, South Burlington, VT 05407. 1-800-344-6336 (FAX 802-864-9846)
www.AandE.com

Ambrose Video Publishing, Inc., 145 W. 45th St., Suite 1115, New York, NY 10036. 1-800-526-4663 (FAX 212 -768-9282)
www.ambrosevideo.com

Facets Multimedia,1517 W. Fullerton Avenue, Chicago, IL 60614. 1-800-331-6197
www.facets.org

Films for the Humanities, P.O. Box 2053, Princeton, NJ 08543-2053. 1-800-257-5126
www.films.com

History Channel (see A&E Home Video)
www.HistoryChannel.com

International Historic Films, Inc., P.O. Box 29035, Chicago, IL 60629. 773-927-2900 (FAX 773-927-9211)
www.ihffilm.com

Kino Video, 333 W. 39th St., Suite 503, New York, NY 10014. 1-800-562-3330 (FAX 212-714-0871)
www.kino.com

Metropolitan Museum of Art, 1000 Fifth Avenue, New York, NY 10028. 212-879-5500 (FAX 212-472-8725)
www.metmuseum.org

Movies Unlimited, 3015 Darnell Road, Philadelphia, PA 19154. 1-800-668-4344
www.moviesunlimited.com

National Archives, National Audiovisual Center, 8700 Edgeworth Drive, Capitol Heights, MD 20743-3701.

New Yorker Video, 16 W. 61st Street, New York, NY 10023. 1-877-247-6200, 212-247-6110
www.NewYorkerFilms.com

PBS Video / Customer Support Center, 1320 Braddock Place, Alexandria, VA 22314-1698 1-800-344-3337 (FAX 703-739-5269)
www.pbs.org

SVE Churchill Media, 6677 N. Northwest Highway, Chicago, IL 60631. 1-800-253-2788 (FAX 1-800-624-1678)
www.svemedia.com

Video Yesteryear, Box C, Sandy Hook, CT 06482-0847. 1-800-243-0987

Zenger Video, 10200 Jefferson Blvd., P.O. Box 802, Culver City, CA 90232-0802. 1-800-421-4246 (FAX 1-800-944-5432)
www.zengermedia.com

Media-Related Web Sites

FEATURE FILM AND VIDEO INFORMATION

*Internet Movie Database: www.imdb.com

Film.com (movie reviews, news, trailers, interviews, showtimes, and more): www.film.com

Movie Studios: www.cs.duke.edu/~fan/movies/makers.html

TV Guide Entertainment Network: www.tvguide.com

*Northwestern University Library: "I Saw It on TV . . .": www.library.northwestern.edu/media/resources/tvguide/tvpubbroad.htm

Yahoo! Movies and Films: dir.yahoo.com/Entertainment/Movies_and_Film

* best sites

ACADEMIC/DOCUMENTARY FILM AND VIDEO

Docuseek Film and Video Finder: www.docuseek.com

Video University (Guide to Public Domain Footage): www.videouniversity.com

Media Reference and Links: www.lib.berkeley.edu/MRC/mediarefmenu.html

*Media Resource Center, University of California, Berkeley: www.lib.berkeley.edu/MRC/level2.html

NICEM AV Producer/Distributor Archive: www.nicem.com/pdurl.htm

*PBS Online: www.pbs.org

* best sites

REVIEWS

American Libraries: Quick Vids**: www.lib.berkeley.edu/MRC/quickvids.html

Booklist**: www.ala.org/booklist/v96/003.html

Bright Lights Film Journal: www.brightlightsfilm.com

Educational Media Reviews Online**: libweb.lib.buffalo.edu/emro/search.html

Inside Out (United Kingdom): www.insideout.co.uk

*MC Journal: The Journal of Academic Media Librarianship**: wings.buffalo.edu/publications/mcjrnl

*MRQE: Movie Review Query Engine: www.mrqe.com

*Roger Ebert on Movies: suntimes.com/ebert/ebert.html

Rotten Tomatoes: www.rottentomatoes.com

Variety: www.variety.com

Video Librarian OnLine**: www.videolibrarian.com

* best sites

**academic/documentary titles

Media-Related Web Sites *(continued)*

FILM HISTORY AND RESEARCH

American Film Institute: **www.AFL.com**

Library of Congress American Memory Project: **memory.loc.gov/ammem/collections/ finder.html**

Midnight Ramble: Early African American Film: **www.moderntimes.com/palace/black/ index.html**

*National Film Preservation Foundation: **www.filmpreservation.org**

News Film Archive at University of Southern California: **www.sc.edu/newsfilm**

Public Motion Picture Research Centers and Film Archives: **lcweb.loc.gov/film/arch.html**

UCLA Film and Television Archive: **www.cinema.ucla.edu**

* best site

COPYRIGHT ISSUES

Copyright Bay: **www.stfrancis.edu/cid/ copyrightbay**

Copyright and Fair Use: **fairuse.stanford.edu**

*The Copyright Website: **www.benedict.com**

U.S. Copyright Office: **lcweb.loc.gov/copyright**

* best site

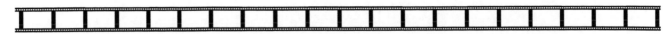

Bibliography

GUIDES TO MEDIA USE

Carnes, Mark C., ed. *Past Imperfect: History According to the Movies*. New York: Owl/Henry Holt, 1996.

Edgerton, Gary R., and Peter C. Rollins. *Television Histories: Shaping Collective Memory in the Media Age*. Lexington, KY: University Press of Kentucky, 2000.

Fraser, George MacDonald. *The Hollywood History of the World*. New York: Beechtree Books, 1988.

Furtaw, Julia C., ed. *The Video Source Book*. Detroit: Gale Research Inc., 1993.

Lacey, Richard. *Seeing With Feeling: Film in the Classroom*. Philadelphia: Saunders, 1972.

Maynard, Richard A. *The Celluloid Curriculum: How to Use Movies in the Classroom*. New York: Hayden Books, 1971.

Moraco, James. *How to Read a Film: The Art, Technology, Language, History, and Theory of Film and Media*. Rev. ed. New York: Oxford University Press, 1981.

O'Connor, John E. *Discussions on Teaching 2: Teaching History with Film and Television*. Washington, DC: American Historical Association, 1987.

O'Connor, John E., ed. *Image as Artifact: Historical Analysis of Film and Television*. Malabar, FL: Krieger, 1989.

O'Connor, John E., comp. *Image as Artifact: Video Compilation*. Washington, DC: American Historical Association, 1988.

O'Connor, John E., and Martin Jackson, eds. *American History/American Film: Interpreting the Hollywood Image*. New York: Unger, 1980.

Rebhorn, Marlettte. *Screening America: Using Hollywood Films to Teach History*. New York: Lang, 1989.

Rollins, Peter C., ed. *Hollywood as Historian: American Film in a Cultural Context*. Lexington, KY: University Press of Kentucky, 1983.

Rosenstone, Robert A. *Visions of the Past: The Challenge of Film to Our Idea of History*. Cambridge, MA: Harvard University Press, 1995.

————, ed. *Revisioning History: Film and the Construction of a New Past*. Princeton, NJ: Princeton University Press, 1995.

Thomas, Tony. *Hollywood and the American Image*. Westport, CT: Arlington House, 1981.

Toplin, Robert Brent. *The Cinematic Historian: Hollywood Interprets America*. Urbana, IL: University of Illinois Press, 1984.

————, intro., *Perspectives on Audiovisuals in the Teaching of History: A Collection of Essays from Perspectives, the Newsletter of the American Historial Association*. Washington, DC: American Historical Association, 1999.

————, *Reel History: In Defense of Hollywood*. Lawrence, KS: University Press of Kansas, 2002.

(continued)

FINDER'S AIDS

Dorsey, William. *The Black Video Guide: Library Edition.* Albuquerque: Video Publications Ltd. and NICEM, 1986.

Hitchen, Howard B., gen. ed. *America on Film and Tape: A Topical Catalog of Audiovisual Resources for the Study of United States History, Society, and Culture.* Westport, CT: Greenwood, 1985.

Leff, Leonard J. *Film Plots: Scene-by-Scene Narrative Outlines for Feature Film Study.* Ann Arbor, MI: Pierian Press, 1983.

Maltin, Leonard. *Leonard Maltin's Movie and Video Guide.* New York: Signet, 2002. (reissued yearly)

Media Log: A Guide to Film, Television, and Radio Programs Supported by the National Endowment for the Humanities. Washington, DC: U.S. Government Printing Office, 1993.

Pratt, Douglas. *The Laser Video Disc Companion.* New York: Zoetrope, 1992.

Reed, Maxine K., ed. *The Video Source Book.* 7th ed. Syosset, NY: National Video Clearinghouse, 2001. (reissued yearly)

Scheuer, Steven H., ed. *Movies on TV and Videocassette.* New York: Bantam, 1993. (issued yearly)

Videohound's Golden Movie Retriever. Detroit: Visible Ink Press, 2002. (updated annually)

GUIDES TO AMERICAN FILM

Abrash, Barbara, and Catherine Egan. eds. *Mediating History: The MAP [Media Alternatives Project] Guide to Independent Video by and About African American, Asian American, Latino, and Native American People.* New York: New York University Press, 1992.

Bogle, Donald. *Blacks in American Films and Television: An Illustrated Encyclopedia.* New York: Simon and Schuster/Fireside, 1989.

Edgerton, Gary R. *Ken Burns' America.* New York: Palgrave/St. Martin's, 2001.

Hardy, Phil, ed. *The Overlook Film Encyclopedia: The Western.* Woodstock, NY: Overlook Press, 1994.

Hitchens, Howard B. gen. ed. *America on Film and Tape: A Topical Catalog of Audiovisual Resources for the Study of United States History, Society, and Culture.* Westport, CT: Greenwood, 1985.

Langman, Larry, and Ed Borg. *Encyclopedia of American War Films.* New York: Garland, 1989.

Marchetti, Gina. *Romance and the "Yellow Peril": Race, Sex, and Discursive Strategies in Hollywood Fiction.* Berkeley: University of California Press, 1993.

May, Lary. *The Big Tomorrow: Hollywood and the Politics of the American Way.* Chicago: University of Chicago Press, 2000.

Rollins, Peter C. and John E. O'Connor, eds. *Hollywood's World War I: Motion Picture Images.* Bowling Green, OH: Bowling Green State University, Popular Press, 1997.

Sayre, Nora. *Running Time: Films of the Cold War.* New York: Dial Press, 1982.

Toplin, Robert Brent, ed. *Oliver Stone's U.S.A.: Film, History, and Controversy.* Lawrence, KS: University Press of Kansas, 2000.

Tracey, Grant. *Filmography of American History.* Westport, CT: Greenwood Press, 2002.

Wetta, Frank J., and Stephen J. Curley. *Celluloid Wars: A Guide to Film and the American Experience of War.* New York: Greenwood, 1992.

Zaniello, Tom. *Working Stiffs, Union Maids, Reds, and Riffraff: An Organized Guide to Films About Labor.* Ithaca, NY: ILR Press, 1996.

Master Index
of Feature Films

Asterisked films are featured in depth in a unit. Other films are synopsized on the indicated page.

Unit 7: World War I

Unit 8: The Twenties

Unit 9: The Great Depression

Unit 12: The Civil Rights Movement

Unit 13: Life in the Fifties and Sixties

Unit 14: The Vietnam War

See complete filmography in Unit 13.

Unit 15: The End of the Twentieth Century

About the Authors

Wendy S. Wilson has been a teacher in the Lexington, Massachusetts, public schools since 1971. She has taught social studies in grades 7–12, has been appointed interim social studies department head, and has served as the cable television specialist systemwide. She also has been a senior lecturer in history at University College, Northeastern University, since 1972; she team-teaches a graduate course on history and media with Gerald Herman as well as an undergraduate course on films of the 1930s. Wilson has been a frequent presenter at national conferences and was the only public-school teacher asked to serve on a task force titled The Historian and Moving-Image Media, which was funded by the National Endowment for the Humanities and the American Historical Association. As a program developer and on-camera presenter, she has hosted three series on an educational satellite network—two on the Columbus Quincentennial and one on U.S. immigration. Wilson is the author of several other Walch publications on social studies topics, including *Daily Warm-Ups: World History* and *Critical Thinking Using Primary Sources in U.S. History.*

Gerald H. Herman is a tenured assistant professor of history and education and a special assistant to the office of the general counsel at Northeastern University. He is the author of a nine-part multimedia presentation and anthology on the culture of World War I titled *World War I: The Destroying Fathers Confirmed* and of award-winning National Public Radio programs—one called *War* on the same subject, and another one on culture of World War II called *The Sound in the Fury.* Herman also has written extensively on history and film, including analyses of individual films, teacher guides for secondary schools and colleges, and bibliographical references (including the media section of *The Craft of Public History* published by Greenwood in 1983). He currently serves as media editor for *The Public Historian.* As a media writer and producer, he created a 40-program instructional television history of Western civilization, *Windows on the Past,* and a video for the National Council on Public History, *Public History Today.* Herman recently published an extensive filmography of dramatic and documentary films about World War I in *Hollywood's World War I: Motion Picture Images* (Peter C. Rollins and John E. O'Connor, eds., Popular Press, Bowling Green State University, 1997). He is currently writing a comprehensive *Historians' Guide to Films.*

We want to hear from you! Your valuable comments and suggestions will help us meet your current and future classroom needs.

Your name_____Date_____

School name_____Phone_____

School address_____

City _____State _____Zip_____Phone number (_____)_____

Grade level taught_____Subject area(s) taught_____Average class size_____

Where did you purchase this publication?_____

Was your salesperson knowledgeable about this product?   Yes_____   No_____

What monies were used to purchase this product?

_____School supplemental budget   _____Federal/state funding   _____Personal

Please "grade" this Walch publication according to the following criteria:

Quality of service you received when purchasing .... A   B   C   D   F

Ease of use.. A   B   C   D   F

Quality of content... A   B   C   D   F

Page layout .... A   B   C   D   F

Organization of material .... A   B   C   D   F

Suitability for grade level .... A   B   C   D   F

Instructional value.. A   B   C   D   F

COMMENTS:_____

_____

What specific supplemental materials would help you meet your current—or future—instructional needs?

_____

Have you used other Walch publications? If so, which ones?_____

May we use your comments in upcoming communications?   _____Yes   _____No

Please **FAX** this completed form to **207-772-3105**, or mail it to:

   Product Development, J. Weston Walch, Publisher, P. O. Box 658, Portland, ME 04104-0658

We will send you a **FREE GIFT** as our way of thanking you for your feedback.   **THANK YOU!**